T0194950

FISHING FOR SOULS

THE RESPONSIBILITY OF EVERY BELIEVER

ALLEN R. RANDLE, SR.

WESTBOW
PRESS®
A DIVISION OF THOMAS NELSON
& ZONDERVAN

WestBow Press books may be ordered through booksellers or by contacting:

WestBow Press
A Division of Thomas Nelson & Zondervan
1663 Liberty Drive
Bloomington, IN 47403
www.westbowpress.com
844-714-3454

Scripture taken from the King James Version of the Bible

ISBN: 978-1-6642-3859-6 (sc)
ISBN: 978-1-6642-3860-2 (hc)
ISBN: 978-1-6642-3858-9 (e)

Library of Congress Control Number: 2021913129

Print information available on the last page.

WestBow Press rev. date: 01/24/2022

Note: The fishing for fish content in this book was written from a freshwater perspective with the use of fresh shrimp as bait. However, the content applies to all types of fish that are caught using the tight-line method with the use of the bait conducive to the target fish.

CONTENTS

Foreword...ix

Acknowledgments..xv

Introduction..xix

Chapter 1   Fishing and Evangelism Are One and the Same 1

Chapter 2   The Prerequisites of Fishing 5

Chapter 3   Methodology Is Everything 8

Chapter 4   The Presentation Matters....................................10

Chapter 5   Fish Bait 13

Chapter 6   Know Where to Fish 14

Chapter 7   Bite Is Really Spelled Bait 16

Chapter 8   Unlimited Possibilities.......................................18

Chapter 9   Fishing the Tight Line.......................................20

Chapter 10   Setting the Hook 28

Chapter 11   Purpose over Problem......................................30

Chapter 12   Keep Your Mind on Your Line 32

Chapter 13   Fishing Never Stops.......................................35

Chapter 14   Hold Your Mouth Right 42

Chapter 15   Fishing by Faith and Works 44

Chapter 16   The Big Mystery 45

Chapter 17   The Calculated Caster....................................46

Chapter 18   Don't Take the Bite for Granted.........................48

Chapter 19   Applying the Drag..49

Chapter 20   You Catch Some and You Miss Some …
             Just Keep Fishing.. 51
Chapter 21   Feeding Is Seeding.. 53
Chapter 22   Twenty-First-Century Fishing Concerns 55
Chapter 23   The Joy of Catching Fish 57
Chapter 24   Catch-'Em, and Then What?................................ 59
Chapter 25   The Dirty Work... 62
Chapter 26   Getting Practical 64
Chapter 27   The Result of All the Effort................................ 65
Chapter 28   The Tackle Box.. 68
Chapter 29   Testimonials 74
             Logan Fields 74
             Mark and Swanzetta Joseph.................................75
             Yardina Wilson...78
             Dianne Jones 80
             Kaitlin Janay Randle 85
             Freddie Banks and Jayvyn Banks: 87
             First Lady Pamela D. Randle................................90

Conclusion 95
About the Author.. 99

FOREWORD

I count it a privilege and an honor to be chosen to write the foreword for a book that I feel will be a blessing to the masses. I have no doubt you will feel all the love and passion that were poured into this book. Pastor Randle has an uncanny way of reaching scholars but making whatever he chooses to say or, in this case, write plain enough for a child to comprehend. After reading this book in its entirety, you will be enlightened on not only the art of fishing but on what it takes to fish for souls.

First Lady Pamela D. Randle

PREFACE

The Five Ws for Fishing for Souls

What?

The world is and always has been in a constant state of chaos and turmoil. Crime manifests itself through gruesome homicides, thefts, and the like. Blood is being shed in the streets and in houses in massive amounts. This is happening though there are churches in almost every neighborhood, and in some places, on every street corner. Imagine what the world would look like today, or what the current state of the human race would look like, had it not been for the presence of the church and the gospel that has brought peace, joy, and hope through salvation and some much-needed stability to an ever-falling world. Imagine how much worse social, spiritual, and emotional states and the condition the world would be had Jesus not made Peter a fisher of men and had Peter not humbled himself, repented of his sins, forsaken his nets, and followed Jesus (Mark 1:16–18).

Today, we the church stand firmly on the gospel as the world crashes down before us, having become the recipients of someone else's fishing efforts. With that said, now imagine what a great place the world would be had believers—the beneficiaries of someone else's catch—truly embraced evangelism and become fishers of men, reciprocating the efforts of those dedicated and focused fishermen. Herein lies the power and powerful effects of what believers have been called to do and be in this world. What we imagine can so easily become a reality if we simply do what we have been called to do, which is to become fishers of men.

Who?

Winning souls to Jesus Christ is the sole responsibility of every professing believer of Jesus Christ, and winning souls requires fishing for souls. Fishing for souls should be the dedicated duty of every believer, considering all believers were once lost fish swimming in a sea of sin until a fisher of men went about his or her duty of fishing for lost souls. Every saved individual shares this testimony: "I was hooked by the gospel." This proves the effectiveness of fishing for souls. Furthermore, and more concretely, fishing for souls is what every believer must do while leaving the outcome of every fishing moment to the Lord of the catch, Jesus Christ, who is in control of all things, including lost souls. Therefore, embrace and enjoy fishing for souls while applying the tips, tactics, truths, and treasures shared in this fishing manual. Experience the success and joy that only fishing for souls can provide, thus fulfilling the Great Commission of Jesus Christ.

When?

Fishing for souls is a *now* moment. Fishing for souls tomorrow has proven time and time again to be too late. For example, fish markets fish today for tomorrow. Fish market owners are always prepared to meet the demands of their clientele, who expect that their fish market will supply their needs. We, the believers, must have the same mindset and sense of urgency to satisfy the command of God as fishers of souls. It's a now moment for no one knows when the Lord will arrive.

Why?

Matthew 28:18–20 is the foundational, fundamental, and underlying reason each professing believer must be a fisher of men:

And Jesus came and spake unto them, saying, All power
is given unto me in heaven and in earth. Go ye therefore,
and teach all nations, baptizing them in the name of the
Father, and of the Son, and of the Holy Ghost: Teaching
them to observe all things whatsoever I have commanded
you: and, lo, I am with you alway, even unto the end of
the world. Amen.

Notice that Jesus issued this mandate to His disciples and to what
would become the church on the day of Pentecost. The mindset that
evangelism should only be confined to the church during the invitation
to Christian discipleship after the sermon is preached must be dismissed.
Each believer must take it upon himself or herself to share the gospel
(to fish for souls). The invitation to Christian discipleship should be that
period of harvest that comes as a result of the work done by the believers—
the church members—while away from the church. In other words, the
members of the church should be setting trotlines all week long. Trotlines
are multiple hooks stretched out along a string that extends across a body
of water. These strings are baited, dropped down into the water, and held
down by heavy weights. They are checked for fish after a few days. The
members should be setting trotlines during the week so that all the pastor
has to do is check the lines for fish at church after the sermon, during the
invitation to Christian discipleship. But outside the worship service, each
believer must take upon himself or herself the responsibility of personally
carrying out the mandate as given in Matthew 28 in obedience to Jesus's
command.

Where?

Matthew 28:19 removes the guesswork concerning the believer's target
audience. "All nations" is plain and clear; it includes all people from
all places, regardless of race, color, or language. When the Holy Ghost
has come upon the believer, the evangelical scope becomes widened to
encompass Jerusalem, Judea, Samaria, and the uttermost part of the earth
(Acts 1:8).

ACKNOWLEDGMENTS

To my beloved father, Nathaniel Randle Sr., who gave me my first fishing experience at the tender age of ten. Daddy, I am honored to have this privilege to acknowledge you as my father and hero, who through investing time, teaching, and love made me the man that I am today. Thank you for showing me the process of how the fish are removed from the water, stored, cleaned, cooked, and enjoyed with the family at the dinner table—the fishing process with a heavenly purpose. These are moments that I will always be grateful for and treasure.

You not only brought my brother and me fishing, you also took the time to teach us the methods and skills involved in fishing. You were also responsible for bringing my mother and my sisters out to the water to fish, giving them the experience of catching fish. Because of you and what the Lord is presently doing through what you have instilled in me, I am fully convinced that the best thing a man can do for his family is to teach them how to fish. What you have done for your family is not only profound, it is prophetic because fishing for souls is every believer's responsibility, whether man or woman.

Daddy, you are responsible for the establishment of my physical and spiritual fishing foundation. And without you and the wholesome experiences I had and still have with you on the water, this book would not be. Daddy, thank you for bringing your little boys fishing. Your leadership, awesome ability to teach, and wisdom have and will lead to the establishment of fishing foundations for many people and the furtherance of the gospel as the information shared in this book will turn ordinary men and women into extraordinary fishermen for souls. The Randle family, the believers, the sinners, the church worldwide, and the kingdom of God are all the better because of you, Daddy.

An ichthyologist is one who studies fish. Daddy, your experience, time dedicated to fishing, and legacy for producing fishermen have earned you honors in our sights. Therefore, on behalf of all the lives impacted and those that will be impacted by your life as a fisherman, it is my prerogative and privilege to call you an ichthyologist. You are, indeed, an ichthyologist in our book, and we say, "Thank you, 'Doctor' Nathaniel Randle Sr."

To my dear friend Pastor Walter August, I did not know what true evangelism was until I met you. I am so grateful to have you in my life and as part of my ministry at the Lighthouse. You are the epitome of the original disciples after the day of Pentecost. Furthermore, your work and church fit the description of what the Lord commanded in the Great Commission. I am so glad to be connected to you and your work. I will continue to pattern my efforts primarily according to the written Word of God, and also according to the living Word of God that I see through your walk and the example you set for all churches to follow through the great work you are doing locally and globally.

Pastor August, you have not only spoken this book into my spirit, you have also been a major contributor to the material in this book. Thank you.

To the Lighthouse Missionary Baptist Church family, you have been more than patient, more than kind, more than understanding, and more than supportive in my efforts to bring glory to the kingdom of God through my writing adventures. You give me the freedoms that I so desperately need as a pastor to become the best pastor I can be. But you also give me the freedoms needed for me to allow my multiple gifts to flow to all the world and to allow my light to shine at its brightest point. Because I just can't wrap my mind around the magnitude of your support nor put my hand on the appropriate words to describe such love and generosity, I'll just say thank you. You can rest assured that it is from my heart.

Lighthouse, God has done it again. We have in our possession a God-inspired work that I believe will revolutionize the evangelical efforts of the church, stabilize the personal witness of the believer, provide the solution for sin for the unbeliever, and give hope to a world in need. Let's take fishing for souls seriously, "both in Jerusalem, and in all Judæa, and in Samaria, and unto the uttermost part of the earth." Lighthouse, let's go fishing!

Last, but certainly not least, to my sweet wife, Pamela Denise Randle. I always knew that you and I had a lot in common, but I never thought in a million years that fishing for fish would be one of those commonalities. You have been my best friend, girlfriend, wife, and so much more. But I would have never imagined that you would be my fishing partner, considering your interest for the thirty-six years I have known you has been clothing and shoes, especially Red Bottoms.

The last four months that you have joined me on the water have been the best time of my life. Who would have thought? I did not know that that type of fun, excitement, fulfillment, and ministry could exist in a marital relationship. The joy we share as we fish together for fish and for souls I will always treasure and hold dear to my heart.

Not only do you make my life complete, you also made this book complete. I could not have written it without you. Thank you for being my wife and my fishing partner. I love you, Pamela.

INTRODUCTION

Now as he walked by the sea of Galilee, he saw Simon
and Andrew his brother casting a net into the sea: for they
were fishers. And Jesus said unto them, Come ye after
me, and I will make you to become fishers of men. And
straightway they forsook their nets, and followed him.

—Mark 1:16–18

This scripture in Mark's gospel classically and uniquely shares solid
evidence with the reader that fishing for fish and fishing for men are one
and the same. By virtue of the fact that Jesus would choose real fishermen
further substantiates this evidence.

Having the evidence is one thing, but making the transition is
another. This has become the struggle for many and the neglect of others.
Simon and Andrew left their physical nets but grabbed hold of their
spiritual nets. They would use their spiritual nets in the same fashion
that they once used their physical nets and began to fish for men. The
church of the living God, which includes every believer—woman and
man, girl and boy, from all walks of life and bearing differing beliefs and
customs—must follow the example of these two disciples, making this
same transition for Jesus's sake.

Somehow the church as a whole has missed the mark, and it has
affected the church and community. Most churches today struggle
with attendance and expanded membership because their members

are simply not fishing. As a result, churches are hindered not only in numerical growth but also in their abilities to provide ministries for the communities in which they serve. The saying, "The more the merrier," is a real thing. The church can simply do more if they have more people and more money. Redirected interests, abilities, and manpower as a result of evangelism can be a mighty force within communities. Doing so can resurrect dead communities and provide booster shots in those communities that need healing and help.

It is an honest oversight by pastors who, for the sake of the ministry and the people they are responsible for, find themselves so consumed with preparing sermons, planning services, and attending social events that they neglect the weightier matter of the gospel: to win souls to Christ. This requires a concentrated and ever-focused effort.

Unfortunately, in most churches the congregation is not being taught the importance, the principles, or the art of fishing for souls. If emphasis were placed on this matter and regular teachings conducted concerning this matter, our churches and communities would be totally different places.

Fishing and Evangelism Are
One and the Same

In Jesus's conversation with Nicodemus concerning salvation and the human struggle with salvation, a clear picture of fishing unfolds. Fishing and evangelism are one and the same.

> For God so loved the world, that he gave his only begotten Son, that whosoever believeth in him should not perish, but have everlasting life. For God sent not his Son into the world to condemn the world; but that the world through him might be saved. He that believeth on him is not condemned: but he that believeth not is condemned already, because he hath not believed in the name of the only begotten Son of God. And this is the condemnation, that light is come into the world, and men loved darkness rather than light, because their deeds were evil. For every one that doeth evil hateth the light, neither cometh to the light, lest his deeds should be reproved. But he that doeth truth cometh to the light, that his deeds may be made manifest, that they are wrought in God. (John 3:16–21)

Let's look at the same scripture in terms of fishing.

> "For God so loved the world"—God so loved and so desired to have fish swimming in a sea of sin.

> "That he gave his only begotten Son"—that He went fishing, casting His Son as bait.

> "That whosoever believeth in him"—that whoever takes the bait.

> "Should not perish"—should be pulled out of the dark, murky, and predatory waters of the world.

> "But have everlasting life"—and be brought to a safe place serving a better and more intentional purpose.

> "For God sent not his Son into the world to condemn the world"—God did not use His Son as bait to cause a problem.

> "But that the world through him might be saved"—but rather to solve a problem.

> "He that believeth on him is not condemned"—those who take the bait will have no regrets having been delivered from a bad place and brought to a better place.

> "But he that believeth not is condemned already"—but those who reject the bait will continue to dwell in regrettable misery in a perishing place.

> "Because he hath not believed in the name of the only begotten Son of God"—because they refused to take the bait.

"And this is the condemnation, that light is come into the world"—and this is the dark result and reality of what happens when the way out is rejected.

"And men loved darkness rather than light, because their deeds were evil"—and so many have rejected the bait because of the familiarity and comfort of the current surroundings and because of the easiness to maneuver in and manipulate their current environments.

"For every one that doeth evil hateth the light"—they would much rather hang onto and hang out in the dark place they are accustomed to than take a chance on change for the better.

"Neither cometh to the light"—and they will ignore the bait, fight the temptation of taking the bait, nibble at the bait, and take the bait with the intent of not getting hooked. Or if hooked, they will resist and fight coming out of their dark setting.

"Lest his deeds should be reproved"—for fear of being exposed after being clothed with what has naturally engulfed them and what they have grown accustomed to all of their lives.

"But he that doeth truth cometh to the light"—but those who take the bait (hook, line, and sinker) come out of darkness seeing that there is a difference between darkness and light.

"That his deeds may be made manifest"—happily and joyfully living a new life with no regrets.

"That they are wrought in God"—yielding to the will, authority, and power of God while fulfilling the purpose that God intended for them from the beginning.

Just as fishing and evangelism are one and the same, fish and people are also one and the same. The world should rejoice and be glad that God, in His infinite mercy, thought enough of humans to make a way for them to come out of sin through His Son, who serves as the source of deliverance through people's evangelistic efforts.

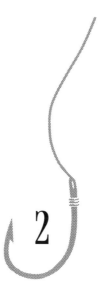

The Prerequisites of Fishing

Just as fishing for fish requires desire, time, patience, and skill, so does fishing for souls. And each of these is an entity and challenge of its own. First, fishing requires desire. Lazy or slothful individuals do not make good fishermen. There must be a strong desire to take the steps necessary to get where the fish are. Getting to the fishing pond is no easy task, especially when considering that the trip will require money, time, and exposure to all the elements of the outdoors. And there's no guarantee of a catch. Therefore, having a desire to go fishing must be motivated and fueled by something deeper. In order to overcome and overlook those things mentioned above, fishermen must be driven by purpose. Purpose is the motivating factor behind desire. Purpose has goals or an expected end that drives an individual beyond obstacles. Though much more will be said about purpose in an upcoming chapter, purpose is the most important factor in getting to the pond.

Desire revolves around and is sparked when believers take into consideration their past lives without Christ, their present lives in Christ, and receive teaching on discipleship and evangelism. Furthermore, the transition from a fish to a fisherman becomes the energy the fisherman needs to propel him or her to fish for souls.

Fishing also requires time, which is the most valuable thing to people. But just like all things require time, fishing for souls must be factored into each day. Ecclesiastes chapter 3 is a reminder that there is a time for all things under the sun. There is also a time to fish for souls. Fishing for souls should be a planned activity or event placed on each person's daily calendar. The concern might be that you need to work or that you have too many other activities in a day. This may be true, but the ideal place to fish is on the job and in other planned activities, since other people are more than likely in those places. Therefore, having time is not the problem; it is taking the time to fish that matters. The only thing that fishing on the job and in daily events requires is having the purpose clearly in mind and a well-thought-out and managed plan.

To a believer who is serious about fishing for souls, water and an opportunity to fish those waters is all he or she sees. I am reminded of a friend who daily carries his rod and reel, bait, tackle, and an ice chest in the back of his truck. He is an opportunist and is always ready to cast his line as he passes bodies of water to and from work and, if time permits, during his lunch break. To him, there is never a wasted moment as long as there are fish in the water. He makes the time to make it happen, and as a result, he is never without fish. This mindset must be employed in each believer's life. We must take our fishing mindsets with us everywhere we go.

Fishing also requires patience. The question that influences patience is, "How badly do you want it?" If one is hungry enough, he or she will do whatever is necessary to appease that hunger. This is where desire further plays a part in the fishing event. The extent of one's past and present thoughts concerning personal salvation, along with gratefulness, drives an uncontrollable hunger that forces the individual to perform a certain behavior that is beyond his or her control. Herein lies patience. It is forced, but it is there. I truly believe that living in freedom, delivered from a life of self-inflicted pains and problems, builds an inner desire to wait patiently through the process of fishing for souls until a change comes.

Fishing for fish or fishing for souls does not require professional skills, but they do require some skill. The skill involved in fishing has more to do with applying the biblical principle of sowing and reaping, as well as Sir Isaac Newton's law of action and reaction. In the great movie *Field of*

Dreams, there is a line that goes, "You build it, and they will come." The same principle applies to fishing. Simply cast the bait out, and the fish will come. Naturally there is a bit more to take into consideration here, which will be discussed in the next chapter, but the principle still applies.

When the fish shows up and bites the line, Newton's law should inevitably take effect. Action is followed by a reaction. Pull in on what's pulling out. It's just that simple.

When fishing for souls, the same principle applies. There must be the use of bait and an apparatus to distribute and/or hold the bait. Then the waiting period—which could be short or long—begins. When the fish takes the bait, the principle takes effect, and the fish is brought into another environment.

Methodology Is Everything

For the advanced fisherman who is serious about fishing for souls, fishing means utilizing methods that involve means and tactics to cause a fish to bite. Though principles are always in effect, successfully landing or catching fish is not automatic. Methods must be applied. Fishermen can afford to miss or not catch dinner, but souls are far too valuable to miss. Since fish do not just jump on the bank or into the boat, methodology is everything.

First of all, using the appropriate bait as a means of catching fish is extremely important. The appropriate bait is determined by the type of fish being fished. For example, not all fish will bite on dead shrimp. Not all fish will bite on live worms. Not all fish will bite on artificial bait. The bait chosen is dependent on the type of fish to be caught.

When fishing for souls, the fisherman must know in advance what attracts the unsaved. The fisherman must know what piques the interests of the unsaved. At that point, efforts are made to present the best bait necessary to lure them to the line.

Additionally, bait is viewed as an investment and will cost the fisherman effort in gathering the bait or money in buying the bait. The true fisherman must be willing to do whatever necessary to find the best bait or to invest in the best bait to ensure fishing success.

The year 1992 is one that I will never forget. At the age of twenty-six, I was a sinner lost in a world of sin. I saw no future, no peace or joy, no money, and no way out. Amid my misery, help came my way through a colleague, Carolyn J. Softly, who extended an invitation to attend her church. I was not very interested in attending the church. But I paid her the courtesy of attending only because she asked. I had already purposed in my heart to a "one and done." To my surprise, she asked again. Only this time, she attached to the invitation a meal after service at a great soul food restaurant. The church I could have passed up, but a meal at this particular restaurant I could not pass up as I was a great fan of soul food, and the meal was free. The same invitation was extended each Saturday, and I willingly accepted. It was not long after that I accepted Jesus Christ as my Savior, was baptized, joined the church, became faithful in every way, became a Sunday school teacher, and joined the church choir and other ministries.

Miracle after miracle have taken place in my personal life and in my family through my relationship and fellowship with the Lord over the next twenty-seven years. Today I am a preaching and teaching pastor of one church in three locations, having fished for and landed thousands of souls all because someone knew how to fish and was willing to invest in the appropriate bait to use in the process.

The tactics involved in catching fish as part of the methodology is found in the next chapter.

4

The Presentation Matters

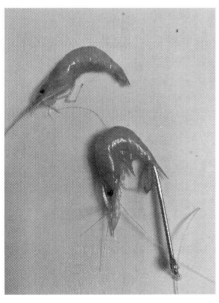

Everyone is familiar with the expression, "The first impression is the everlasting impression." Even furniture store managers base their marketing strategies on how well they display their products. These marketing strategists invest unlimited amounts of money to ensure a proper presentation of their products because they believe that; it is a fact that presentation matters. With what the line is baited and how well the line is baited make a tremendous difference before the line hits the water. This fishing tactic will determine whether there will be a successful catch and the length of time it will take to get a bite.

For example, when using shrimp, it is best to use ones with their heads still attached because fish are attracted to the heads. The fish will pursue the body of the shrimp as well, but they will attack the head first. Therefore, when fishing with a shrimp with the head on, it is best to place the shrimp on the hook by placing the hook through the tail end first and sliding the tip of the hook through the body until the tip of the hook lands in the head of the shrimp. If between casts the bait loses its position or becomes half eaten, it is always best to replace the bait. It is an intricate and most times tedious routine, but it is worth it for the presentation matters.

Just the same, when fishing for souls, the presentation matters. There is a presentation that must be maintained at the church and in our personal lives.

The church's presentation must be above reproach, excellent, and bear the appearance of perfection in the public's eye. It is, after all, the house of God. Nothing about God and what His name is associated with or attached to should be substandard. Rather, it should be exceedingly glorious in appearance. This applies to the inside of the building and the outside, including the landscape. The appearance of the church should be nothing short of breathtaking.

The believer's personal life presents another form of presentation. Believers' personal lives speak without saying words. What the believer looks like personally or how the believer carries himself says much to the public about personal public presentation. So it matters what believers wear, how their hair looks, and how they manage other personal affairs and belongings. Believers should make every effort to present themselves well, thus making themselves highly attractive to lost souls. If lost souls find the believer attractive, they will come asking the question, "What must I do to be saved?"

The previous paragraph stresses the importance of personal presentation from an outer perspective. But there is another form of presentation that is just as important, if not more important. This presentation focuses on the inner person and the unseen. Love, joy, peace, and hope cannot be seen or touched in a physical sense, but they can be felt in a spiritual sense. This presentation is very attractive to unbelievers because it appeals to that which every person craves. Jesus Christ is the foundation and explanation of this presentation through salvation and is the only one who can satisfy the spiritual craving of a soul that is void of love, joy, peace, and hope.

With this view of truth, the believer must realize that he or she has what sinners need and should be highly concerned with the inner presentation. For when the inner presentation and the outer presentation can clearly be seen by the unbeliever, the believer's life becomes even more attractive and alluring.

Even the very words spoken from the believer's mouth contributes to the presentation. Matthews 12:34b says, "out of the abundance of the heart, the mouth speaks." The believer's heart should be filled with the joy of salvation, which tempers the believer's thoughts and spoken words. The believer's words are seasoned with salt and minister medicine to the lives of the lost.

Proverbs 18:21a says, "death and life are in the power of the tongue." The believer ministers life into other people's lives. This life can and will lead to eternal life for the lost or unsaved.

Then there is a peculiar attitude, temperament, perseverance, patience, and humility that are clearly present in the believer and cannot be comprehended, explained, or duplicated but ever desired by the unbeliever. This is yet another aspect of the Christlike presentation that makes the believer extremely attractive.

5

Fish Bait

It is a fact that fish bite on fish. Whether in freshwater lakes or ocean saltwater, fish bite on fish. It could be the smell or the taste of the fish that attracts other fish. One will never know, but one thing for certain is that fish eat fish.

As it relates to fishing for souls or catching people who are like us, it would make sense that those being fished for would be attracted to those who look like and have much in common with them. Fishermen of souls must see themselves as fish bait, having been saved and bearing the marks, appearance, signs, and scent of Jesus Christ. They should not place themselves above others. Instead, they should meet people where they are and make themselves available for others as they have already gone through what others presently encounter. Sinners should feel uncomfortably comfortable around believers. And believers must know that they have something worthwhile to offer the sinner. As fish bait, believers must realize that they are the sinners' way out of their miserable, sinful conditions.

6

Know Where to Fish

Knowing where to fish is extremely important. Though fish are always biting, fish don't always bite well in every body of water. Fish inhabit bodies of water that are conducive to their likes. Fish must feel comfortable in their environments, so they will find environments or bodies of water that make them feel good and provide adequate food for them. The smart fisherman is a wise and educated fisherman that takes this in account.

This fisherman also knows that water depth, water color, and water temperature are extremely important, and all of these have a direct bearing on fish habitat. The smart fisherman knows the vegetation found in a specific body of water. The smart fisherman also knows what type of floor is found in the body of water, whether it is a soft bottom or a hard bottom. Finally, the smart fisherman knows how the seasons affect the fish habitat, and he or she makes adjustments accordingly.

When fishing for souls, the fisherman must seek lost souls in places where those souls are most comfortable and frequent most often. This requires education and keen observation. People are most comfortable at work, the grocery store, the barbershop, the beauty salon, sporting events, and in their homes. Meeting people where they are comfortable and frequent the most is the strategy the fisherman must employ to have success. The smart fisherman must show up and cast the bait in their direction, where they are. If the lost soul does not take the bait the first time, sooner or later he or she will. Just keep fishing!

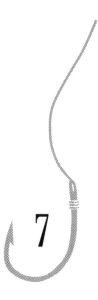

7

Bite Is Really Spelled *Bait*

An empty hook gets no attention. If much time elapses between casts, it is because there is no bait on the line. My motto is, "When in doubt, check it out." If the line sits in the water over an extended period without any action, there is a good chance that the hook is empty. Reel in the line, and check it out. Time is fish; never babysit an empty hook.

It was alluded to earlier in this book that the bait's presentation matters, suggesting that the bait is the leading factor and driving force in catching fish. I plainly state and reemphasize this matter regarding the church as stated in chapter 1 that Jesus Christ is the bait. Failure to fish with Jesus is the detriment and downfall of the church and renders each believer's fishing efforts null and void. As a matter of fact, churches that are not taking in many members could be suffering from fishing with no bait, a bad presentation, or the use of the wrong bait. The latter needs further attention.

Fishing with the wrong bait is a common problem in fishing. There are generally two types of bait. One is real live or dead bait; the other is artificial bait. The fish know the difference, and most fish prefer live or dead real bait opposed to artificial bait. However, if presented properly, certain fish, called game fish—such as freshwater bass and sac-a-lait or saltwater trout and red snapper—will bite on artificial bait. Be mindful that artificial bait is just a highly engineered representation or facsimile of live or dead real bait and does not have the scent of live bait. The success factor in using this bait depends on how well the fisherman works it in effort to make the bait look real or alive to lure the fish to the hook, which is slightly located inside the bait.

The use of artificial bait has been a leading factor in the numerical and spiritual growth of many churches. Unfortunately, many people are lured into the church but do not stay long once they discover the deception that was used to get them into the church, or when they discover that those who led them to the church were fake.

Church members should make every attempt be like Jesus and be real just like Jesus. With Jesus as the bait, there will be a sure bite and good results to follow.

Furthermore, be certain that the bait used can entertain a date because again, presentation is everything. In other words, make certain that the bait used is properly secured to the hook. During the cast, the bait has a tendency to adjust for the worst. Therefore, the line should be cast with much gentle care and consideration to ensure that the bait stays situated on the hook and remains presentable to the fish. The goal is for the bait to attract a fish. The bait should be so well situated on the hook that it causes the fish to hang around and date the bait. Failure to do this could become a missed opportunity to land a good or a big fish. For this reason, fishermen must give the fish a reason to entertain the bait and maintain interest in the bait.

The same applies to the church and every fishing believer who is seeking to fish for souls. Loosely handling the gospel and how the gospel is laid on the line—presented—determine the outcome of the witnessing experience. Every good fisherman knows his or her trade. The believer who fishes for souls must know his or her trade as well. Priority must be placed on the Gospels of Jesus Christ as the bait having a presentation that is second to none. Remember, actual fish have no heaven or hell to consider at life's end, but people do.

8

Unlimited Possibilities

Fish are always biting, but we are not always fishing. When good habits and education are applied to fishing, they together can yield great results and unlimited possibilities. Studying the fish's habits and routines is always helpful in catching fish, but considering one's personal fishing habits and routines are equally as important.

To fish and fishing require action. According to the *Merriam Webster Dictionary*, fish (as a verb) means to attempt to catch fish, to seek something by roundabout means, to search for something under water, and to engage in a search by groping or feeling.

Fishing is the present act of doing the above.

At any rate, to fish and fishing require actions or activities being involved in the process.

Though there are exceptions, fish will not bite unless they are attracted to the bait. Fishing is usually a "make it happen" type of event, and the catch lies in the hands of the one who is willing to put forth the effort.

Fishing presents unlimited possibilities in the size and number of the fish caught. Both depend on how well the bait is worked. When fishing with a live worm or an artificial worm, the fisherman must cause the worm to take on the characteristics or actions of a worm. The same thing applies to the use of grasshoppers, frogs, or other bait. The action of the bait rests in the hands of the fisherman. What this teaches is that he or she who fishes for souls must be real or appear real. Those who don't know the Lord live in a world of fake and false and need something and someone that is real. Christianity is alive, real, and well. And that is what every soul longs to possess. Therefore, the believer must present this realness in such a way that it becomes attractive, desirable, available, and attainable.

When the fisherman considers his or her fishing habits and routines, the fisherman must also be willing to come out of the comfort zone and make the necessary investments to bring about good results. This may entail the fisherman having to go to where the fish are biting. Certain seasons, water depth, water temperature, and water color are all factors that will determine where the fish are located and whether the fish can be fished from the bank or from a boat. If by boat, then buying a boat will become the necessary investment and cost the fisherman. The serious fisherman will make this investment.

The believers who are serious about fishing for souls are willing to make the necessary investments to increase their abilities to win souls. These fishermen will invest their time and finances in seminars, workshops, conferences, literature, and study tools to increase their chances to win souls, which will open many doors of unlimited opportunities for both the fisherman and the won soul.

9

Fishing the Tight Line

There are different types of fishing. There is game fishing, which predominantly entails fishing with artificial bait requiring the use of multiple castings to lure the fish to the line. There is trotline fishing, which entails setting and baiting multiple hooks on a single line positioned in an open body of water and left for a few days. The fish simply hooks itself in this style of fishing. The customary bait used is dead real bait. There is jug fishing, which is similar to trotline fishing. With this type of fishing, plastic gallon jugs are attached to a short string with a baited hook and a heavy weight at the end of the string. They are then tossed into a body of water and checked periodically for results. Then there is tight-line fishing. Tight-line fishing is the most common form of fishing for the average fisherman who is not fishing for the fun or the sport of it but rather to put food on the table. It entails the use of a rod and reel and the capability of casting the line a long distance in a desired direction. The line is baited with live real bait of many types common to the fish's water environment, including shrimp, shads, shiners, small crawfish, worms, and grasshoppers. A heavy one-ounce or two-ounce weight is attached at the end of the line, about a foot or so above or below the hook.

The hook and weight configuration varies among fishermen, though

I believe the former is more effective because in this configuration, the bait has freedom to move about the water, giving the impression of having life. In tight-line fishing, after the bait is cast into the water, the fisherman makes certain that the line has no slack in it after the weight lands at the very bottom of the water—hence tight-lining. Once the line is tight, with little or no slack in it, the fisherman waits patiently for the fish to come to the bait. If the bait is appropriate, attractive, and the presentation is right, the fish will come. Though all these methods are proven effective ways to catch fish, for the sake of this book and its purpose, this chapter focuses on tight-line fishing, which is best associated

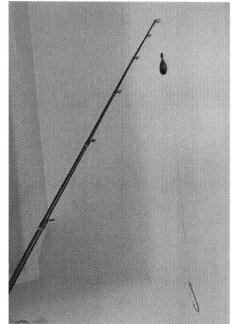

with the church and the believer who fishes for souls.

There is an art to tight-line fishing. This section of the book for the serious fisherman or fisherwoman is the most critical; therefore, give diligent attention to the following information. This section has the power to transform the fishing experience and sinners' lives forever. Remember, fishermen live for the bite. It's all about the bite.

I have been tight-line fishing for roughly forty-four years, and I have encountered every type of bite there is. I have even caught fish oddly, with the string wrapped around the fish's body without ever getting the hook inside its mouth. However the fish are caught, the ultimate goal is simply to catch them.

There are different types of bites associated with tight-line fishing. For the sake of this book, I have taken the liberty to name them myself. There is what I have termed as the smackdown-takedown. With this type of bite, the fish does not take the time to date the bait. The fish simply sees the bait and in one motion and effort, takes the bait and swims away with it, causing the tip of the rod to pull downward and forcefully leaving the fisherman no choice but to pull upward. This upward pull sets the hook in the fish's mouth, making it difficult for the fish to escape. Then the fish is reeled in. Usually there is a 100 percent chance of catching this fish.

There are souls who will come to Christ in exactly same way as described above. They will not waste any time. They will come to Jesus with their minds made up and will join the ministry, following all the necessary steps to do so. They usually are extremely faithful and dependable and will hold up as a faithful witness and provide a steady, true Christian example for others to follow. This individual basically hooks himself.

Then there is the thump'n' bite action. With this type of bite, the fish chews on the bait and, with a side-to-side motion of its body, intermittently pulls the line. Knowing when to jerk or set the hook is always the question and becomes a judgment call for the fisherman. The tip of the line repeatedly bobs upward and then downward until the bait is removed from the hook. There must be an appropriate timing of one of the thumps in order to pull the line and set the hook. Jerking the line prematurely must be avoided. It is always best to pull or jerk the line, setting the hook on any one of the downward thumps or pulls. Carelessness and overaggressiveness, including proper concentration and timing, could cost the fisherman a big catch. The success rate of catching the fish is high when done properly.

When fishing for the soul that demonstrates the thump'n' action, the fisherman must concentrate and track the actions of the individual. It usually takes this type a while to make up his or her mind. They repeatedly visit the church but are hesitant about making a decision. They show promising signs that they are ready, but often they are not. Moving too fast could cause a missed opportunity. Moving too slowly could also cause a missed opportunity. The fisherman must perfectly time the actions of the individual and use wisdom and certain behavior patterns as a way of determining the right time to make a move.

Then there is the slack-and-pull bite. With this type of bite, the fish pushes the bait toward the fisherman, causing slack in the line. If the slack is not removed by slowly reeling in the line, the fish will take the bait without the fisherman detecting it. Therefore, keeping the line tight keeps the fisherman aware of what the fish is doing with the bait at all times. When the fish gives slack, the fish is literally affixing the bait in its mouth while moving in the direction of the fisherman. And more often than not, the next step is a sudden forceful pull down. This sudden pull down should be followed by a jerk of the rod while setting the hook firmly in the fish's mouth. Usually there is a 100 percent chance of catching this fish.

These individuals are those who pursue the gospel. They are the ones who are literally moving in the right direction, but it is difficult to tell because there seems to be no concrete indication that they are. They give the impression that they are giving up, but they are actually moving closer to making a decision and a commitment. They are soaking up the fellowship and eating up the gospel. But it is often difficult to detect. Then suddenly, at an unexpected time, they join the church. This unexpected moment and the element of surprise is usually accompanied by much rejoicing by all parties involved.

Then there is the tap-tap-tap bite. This is the most difficult bite to discern. It is as though the fish is indecisive. It is as though the fish is going back and forth in a hesitant and suspect way. The tip of the line moves periodically, and it appears from the surface of the water that there is never constant contact with fish and hook. This type of bite requires much concentration, imagination, and timing. If timed right, there is a 50 percent chance of catching this fish.

With the tap-tap-tap individual, there is an annoyance that comes with it. Though this bite is annoying, it must be handled with care because there is no way of telling how promising this individual is. It could be a "small fish," or it could be a "big fish." A small fish is young and immature in the faith, and probably will not immediately make a major impact in the church. The big fish has the potential to affect the church profoundly in every aspect of the word "faithful." Therefore, the tap-tap-tap must be treated with top care because this fish could represent the nibble of an extremely inexperienced small fish that just cannot seem to grip the bait, or it could be a huge fish operating with wisdom and strategy to take the bait off the hook.

Two months ago I landed a twenty-pound and thirty-six-inch flathead catfish that bit the hook like a one-ounce goldfish with that little tap-tap-tap action. I decided to reel in the hook, thinking that the bait was gone.

But much to my surprise, as I reeled it in, there was a massive jerk on the line. Approximately five minutes later, after playing tug-of-war with that huge fish, I finally landed it. Below is a picture and further reason why tap-tap-tap bites must be taken seriously. The meat from that one fish completely filled three large bowls.

Then finally there is the first stage of the bite, the point of initial contact, called the nibble. The nibble is the fish's first encounter with the bait and deserves the fisherman's undivided attention. At this point the fisherman enters into a concentrated quiet zone of preparedness as he or she anticipates the fish's next move and the plan of response. The fisherman plasters his or her eyes on the tip of the line and the string but makes no sudden move. Usually within a matter of seconds after the initial contact, the fish will make the next move. That will dictate the fisherman's next course of action. Please understand that setting the hook in the fish's mouth is nearly impossible during the nibble. The fisherman should exercise extreme patience in this phase and not jerk the line prematurely. The truth is that there is no telling what's on the other end of the line. It could be a small sandwich-size fish about a foot long, or it could be a large fish of three feet in length with the capability of supplying enough fish to feed a family reunion. It is advised to just let the nibble materialize into something more concrete. After the nibble, there will be one of the previously mentioned bites or an empty hook cleared by a clever fish. Just for the record, with patience, the fisherman will eat more fish than the fish will eat bait.

In evangelism and fishing for souls, the nibble can materialize into either the beginning of a glorious relationship or a missed opportunity. The potential new convert, candidate for baptism, or new member of the church must be handled with the same care and consideration given to actual nibbling fish. Because it is the individual's first encounter with Jesus who is the bait, the individual deserves the fisherman's undivided attention. And just like the fish, the fisherman enters a concentrated quiet zone of preparedness while anticipating the individual's next move and his or her own response. The fisherman plasters his or her eyes on the individual but makes no sudden move. Within a matter of time after the initial contact, the individual will likely make the next move, which will dictate the fisherman's next course of action. Please understand that getting the slightest commitment is nearly impossible during this phase of contact. The fisherman should exercise extreme patience in this phase, not take anything for granted, or respond prematurely. Patience is required here because, the truth is, there is no telling what is on the other end of the line. It could be one who will sit, soak, and sour on the pews of the church. Or it could be a very faithful and committed individual who will do great things in the church and community. Because the unknown exists, it is advised to just let the nibble materialize into something more concrete. If it does, be grateful and thank God for it.

Many times the nibble will lead to an empty hook. As the old saying goes, "You can't catch them all." This is so true, even when fishing for souls. So many times what starts out to be so promising will lead to another missed opportunity. Know that it is all part of fishing, and it happens to everybody, even the more experienced fishermen. The truth of the matter is that the fisherman, who is at a great disadvantage, has a blind view of the underwater activity and no control over the fish and its underwater activity. The fisherman can only react to what the fish does. The odds of catching fish are stacked up against the fisherman before he or she casts the line. Therefore, the fisherman should rejoice whether a fish is landed or when opportunities are missed.

It is no different with souls. Most of the time the moment looks so promising, the groundwork for success properly established, but the effort is unfruitful. But do understand that just like the fisherman for fish, the fisherman for souls is always at a great disadvantage based on what the evangelist cannot see or does not know. Many times when I am fishing I properly set the hook, but before I can pull the fish out of the water, it maneuvers itself around an underwater log, gets caught up in underwater seaweed or brush, and causes a missed opportunity. In the fishing and natural worlds, the same phrase is used, "caught up." People we fish for do the very same thing. They purposely or inadvertently get caught up, wrapped up, or tied up in their own worlds or natural environments and cause what could have been a great opportunity to turn into a missed one. Even in this, the fisherman must be grateful and never get discouraged. Keep fishing because ultimately, some things are beyond the fisherman's control.

I conclude this segment with another side of the nibble. Rather than information, I call it "nibblemation."

There are individuals who will nibble but never take the bait. These are the ones who will give the impression that they are going to accept Christ or even join the church, but they never do. They never commit to anything. They just hang around. The best thing to do is reset the bait. In actual fishing, resetting the bait is simply reeling the line in about two to three feet, giving another fish an opportunity at the bait. This usually works as the movement of the bait attracts other fish. Fishers of men should always be willing to perform a reset, thus making Jesus accessible and available to all.

It is also wise for every fisherman of fish to be extremely knowledgeable of the nibble. This knowledge is usually developed over much time and experience, and it has proven to be a priceless and valuable asset to the fisherman. What appears to be a nibble may not be a nibble. Know the nibble and the nature or source of the nibble. What first appears to be a fish nibble often turns out to be the activity of other undesirable water species, such as crabs. Be proactive because desirable fish always nibble with the intent of doing something more serious, but crabs take the bait in their claws and ward off a potential fish.

When fishing for men, this same wisdom and knowledge must be applied to the nibble. Some people will purpose in their hearts to waste the evangelist's time. They are undesirables only in the sense that they cannot bring further increase to the kingdom of heaven because they, in their saved states, draw attention to themselves, being highly inconsiderate of others because of selfishness or because of extreme ignorance of the evangelistic process and mandate. Therefore, they will consciously or unconsciously disable the evangelist in his or her efforts to bring more nonbelievers into the kingdom of God.

All the forms of fish bites discussed apply to fishing for fish and for souls. To guarantee good fishing success, make certain that the presentation is good, be patient, and know the bite.

Why is it important to know how fish bite? It is important because people bite exactly the same way.

- If believers fish properly, some unbelieving potential converts and church members will accept Jesus by way of smackdown-takedown.
- If believers fish properly, some unbelieving potential converts and church members will take Jesus by way of a thump'n' bite.
- If believers fish properly, some unbelieving potential converts and church members will take Jesus by way of tap-tap-tap bite.
- If believers fish properly, some unbelieving potential church members will become attracted to Jesus, giving the believer another opportunity to bring in a soul.

Now take a moment and imagine if the believer did not fish at all. What damaging and deadly effects that would have on sinners, families, and communities! When believers hold back or fail to cast the bait that was guaranteed to change lives or that was responsible for rescuing them from a sea of sin, there is no help or hope for a perishing world that will one day be consumed and engulfed in flames at the end of this world on the Lord's command.

10

Setting the Hook

Setting the hook is more than likely the most important aspect of catching a fish. Without setting the hook, the fish cannot be brought out of the water. When the fisherman senses the proper time to jerk the line, he or she quickly and sharply jerks the line upward with confidence that the fish had an opportunity to get a good bite on the bait. If the fisherman guesses wrongly or misjudges the bite, the jerk is futile. But if the fisherman times the bite properly, the hook becomes lodged somewhere in the fish's mouth as shown in the picture above.

The setting of the hook during the jerk causes the rod to bend. This bending is not only important, it is also exhilarating. Fishermen live for this moment. It is addicting. The initial bending of the line is also a good determiner of the size of the fish on the line. The next phase—the reeling in of the fish—which takes place immediately after setting the hook, heightens the exhilaration. More information will be shared on this subject in an upcoming chapter.

In the same way, the most important, exciting, and exhilarating part about winning a soul to Christ is the sinner's initial surrender to Jesus, which is the setting of the hook. This is the moment when God's mercy and grace gift of salvation are actively seen in the sinner's life. The sinner takes the bait, and the hook is set in the heart of the believer, bringing the individual into a new life of blissful change through Jesus Christ and eventually to eternal life in the kingdom of God.

Immediately thereafter, and as part of the redemptive process, the sinner is led through the prayer of salvation, which is the "bending rod" moment that serves to further heighten the soul-winning event. The bending is that initial exciting and thrilling moment of bearing witness to that saved soul coming out of darkness and moving into the marvelous light. The joy of the success is felt during and after properly setting the hook. Then more unexplainable feelings surface that boost the fisherman's adrenaline unlike anything else. Higher levels of joy seem to occur between the bending of rod and the reeling in of the fish. This joy-filled moment gives the fisher of men an overwhelming feeling of excitement knowing that another soul has been delivered from the destructive forces of the world and a burning hell and won for the kingdom of God.

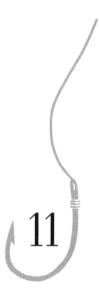

11

Purpose over Problem

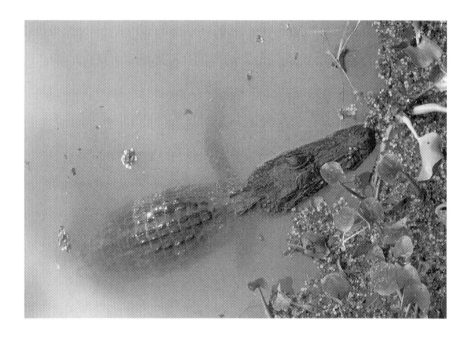

Fishing is usually an outdoor event whether it is fishing for fish or for souls. Snakes, alligators, mosquitoes, flies, and inclement weather can always become influencing factors that could determine one's level of commitment.

Fishermen can't be afraid of snakes. Water snakes are known to hang around water. Some people believe that seeing snakes in the water is a sure sign that the fish are biting. The jury is still out on that one. When a fisherman's purpose is clearly defined and established, it does not matter what stands in the way. This individual will tread over the vile and vicious creatures of this earth to accomplish the mission. I am reminded of my uncle and his brother who, as young fishermen, knew where the fish were biting. They knew of a guaranteed place to catch fish, but they had to deal with many snakes to get to there. Because they were determined and had made up their minds that they would not allow anything to stop them, they were willing to deal with the snakes. After all, that which has the potential to pose problems must be overcome by having a bigger purpose.

First, fear should never be a factor when fishing for souls. Fear of anything when fishing for souls should not thwart the fisherman's purpose. If fear or uncomfortable feelings become a factor due to problems, a good opportunity will be lost. Expect problems to come as a fisher of souls knowing that as Christ overcame the world through His death, burial, and resurrection, you have already overcome the world as well. Stay focused on the purpose.

Fishermen of souls must be aware of the predators that exist in the form of the devil, whose job is to steal, kill, destroy, discourage, and derail evangelistic plans. One must consider what Jesus had to go through to get to Mount Calvary and to the right hand of the Father. It took much agony, pain, suffering, bloodshed, and even death to accomplish His redemptive goal. Jesus was victorious because His purpose was bigger than His problem. We must be willing to weather the elements that be in order to win a soul. It won't be easy, but it is never impossible when Jesus is factored in and is the example.

12

Keep Your Mind on Your Line

When fishing for fish or for souls, concentration is extremely important. It could be the difference between rejoice and regret.

When fishing for fish, distractions of all types will occur. Naturally, nature will play its part as will natural human interactions when fishing with others. But the most distracting of all are the fish that repeatedly jump out of the water and then back into the water. Most of the time these distractions are caused by the fish called the mullet, which are hardly ever caught by way of rod and reel. The mullets are the entertainers of the water and should not be given any attention.

However, there are other huge and more desirable fish that create a tremendous splash in the water near the fisherman. This could be a very distracting experience, especially when the fish are biting slowly or those being caught are very small, but the fisherman has high hopes of catching the big one. There is nothing more exhilarating than seeing a huge fish near the surface and literally out of the water. The problem that usually occurs is that of the fisherman becoming distracted and sometimes discouraged when big fish are clearly seen and heard on the surface of the water, but there seems to be inactivity on the bottom of the water and no bites on the line. It is possible to get so caught up in hoping and dreaming about catching the big fish that looking away from one's own line and business occurs with regularity, causing the fisherman to neglect the business at hand.

The same thing happens with fishers of men. Fishermen, it is possible to get so caught up in the peripheral that the matter at hand becomes neglected. Fishing for men requires maximum focus and concentration, and that focus and concentration should not be jeopardized by what happens around the fisherman. People with no good intent could be a major distraction to those with major potential. What should matter most is what transpires below the water for the fisherman who is fishing deep below the surface. These huge surface swimmers should only serve to encourage, motivate, and inspire the fisherman to focus on his or her own line because it only takes one moment for the fish to take the bait without the fisherman even being aware of it.

Those who fish for men should recognize the value of focus and concentration and not overly concern themselves with outside activities that are irrelevant to the matter at hand. Irrelevant activity when fishing for men also includes focusing on what other people are doing rather than monitoring one's own business.

On one occasion my wife and I ventured out to our favorite fishing spot. For whatever reason, I gave her line more attention than I gave mine, and my line sat propped up, unmanned, on the side of the boat. I was waiting for the big hit, and it came suddenly. Wow, did it come suddenly! Not only that, it was also dramatic, as the fish nearly pulled my rod and reel completely out of the boat. The rod made screeching sounds as it scraped along the fiberglass boat deck. It came so suddenly, that I, in a feeble and desperate act of saving my line, did not have enough time to grab the line and properly set the hook in the fish's mouth. The most agonizing part of it all was that I did have the opportunity to reel the fish in for approximately five seconds, which gave me the opportunity to feel the weight of the fish before it broke the line. The thrill and joy only lasted about five seconds before disappointment came. I have no doubt that the fish weighed anywhere in the neighborhood of twenty to thirty pounds.

But that is not all. I have since had to deal with the thoughts of what could have been had I just given proper attention to my line. That moment created an empty feeling within that sometimes surfaces to this day. And I must admit that the very thought of the experience is sometimes hauntingly terrorizing.

The people we as believers are fishing for are loaded with spiritual, life-changing potential. All of them matter and should be treated as "big fish," the prize catch. Therefore, when fishing for men, give proper attention to each of them. Give them undivided attention for in the sight of God, they are the "big catch."

13

Fishing Never Stops

Just for the record, and for the sake of clearing the minds of the world's view of fishing for fish, fishing today is not what God intended it to be about in the beginning. In the beginning, fishing was always a means of providing food for the table. In today's society, fishing has become more of a sport, where caught fish are weighed and recorded, and the fisherman is awarded a prize. The real purpose of fishing for fish has diminished over time. God never intended for fish to be thrown back into the water. They are to be kept and used for food. If not kept, fish should be given away as a source of food for someone else.

And the same thing has happened among believers in their quest to fish for souls.

Every believer or fisher of souls must reconnect to God's true intent for fish and fishing for souls, start afresh today, and never stop fishing. Fishermen must fish at all houses: the schoolhouse, the jailhouse, the White House, and their own houses. The fisherman must fish all places: the grocery store, ball parks, recreational parks, movie theaters, and all other places where there are people. Every encounter with a human soul should be a fishing experience of some sort for the believer, the fisher of souls.

Fishermen for souls should never stop fishing. Whether in town or out of town, fishing never stops. There are times when out of town or out of state on vacation that believers will have opportunities to witness for Jesus and share the plan of salvation. Or at the very least, sow the seed of salvation in lives of others or water the seeds that someone else planted. When the opportunity comes, believers should take advantage of those opportunities and allow God, in His own time and according to His own plan for those individuals' lives, to give the increase. Believers do not know where others are regarding salvation, but God does. It is a truism, however, that God is always working and moving in people's lives, and so should believers. When the spiritual connection is made through sowing or watering, God, who gives the increase, will lead that individual to the next step. If the recipient of the sown seed lives close enough to the sower or waterer, the recipient will usually seek out that person, his or her church, and God. If there is much distance between the sower or waterer and the seed recipient, the recipient usually asks about next steps or the appropriate church to attend to further facilitate and accommodate what God did in the new convert. If there is no inquiry, the sower or waterer should at least assist the recipient in finding a church and pastor in the city in which he or she lives.

I am reminded of what I was told concerning bass when they are released after bass tournaments. The bass that are caught during the tournaments are kept alive in compartments of boats called live wells until the end of the tournament. With the exception of some prize fish, of course, the other fish are released back into the water. Interestingly, those released fish usually do not venture far from the place where they received their liberty. The place of their freedom becomes their new habitat. I would not have believed it had I not witnessed it. It's as though once the fish had a taste of freedom, they no longer had a desire to return to the dark and deep. To this day, bass can be found alive and swimming alongside boat landings, especially days and weeks after tournaments. This should be the experience for every new convert once the seed of salvation has been sown and planted and God has given the increase. Believers must do their parts to assist and facilitate the process and never stop fishing.

As it relates to fishing for souls when out of town, on an elevator, or in any of the previously mentioned houses or places, what does that look like or sound like? This question is usually the million-dollar one for all fishermen. First and foremost, as it relates to what fishing for souls in these venues looks like, the fisherman must realize that there is never a disconnect from fishing. Second, the fisherman must realize that there must be readiness at all times. Third, the fisherman must be looking for fishing opportunities. Those who love fishing always bring their fishing equipment with them wherever they go, even out of town. Even though the out-of-town fisherman does not intend to keep the fish, he or she still enjoys the moment and engages in the experience. The easy part of the experience is that when fishing for souls, fishermen are sowing or watering the seed of salvation and does not have to concern themselves with the cleaning process. They simply catch them and give them away; they literally contribute to another's harvest by doing the legwork. This is what fishing out of town looks like.

As it relates to what fishing for souls when out of town sounds like, it has a language. There is an unspoken language called letting the light shine. It simply entails the fisherman for souls walking in the spirit of God. Walking in the spirit of God is when the Bible can be seen clearly in the believer through his or her actions, mannerisms, and communication with others, such as waiters and waitresses at restaurants, desk attendants and housekeepers at hotels, and window workers at drive-thru restaurants. This nonverbal fisherman always realizes the value of second- and third-party encounters. He or she realizes the great influence and highly monitors thoughts, actions, and words because the fisherman knows that they carry weight and that others, whether second parties or third parties, are observing them.

Believers give off spiritual vibes that cannot be explained or seen with the naked eye, but they can be felt deep down in one's innermost being. Again, it cannot be seen because it is spiritual. This nonverbal behavior usually sparks conversations that open the door for the believer to sow the seed of salvation further or water the seed already sown. This could lead to that decisive moment when the individual is introduced to the gospel story, along with the plan and prayer of salvation as they engage in the very act of salvation. Never stop fishing because fish are always biting. Salvation and rejoicing are always the result. Luke 15 speaks well to that final statement. Read the following passage, and share in the rejoicing of those who suffered loss but had a reason to rejoice in the end. Also take notice of heaven's response.

> Then drew near unto him all the publicans and sinners for to hear him. And the Pharisees and scribes murmured, saying, This man receiveth sinners, and eateth with them. And he spake this parable unto them, saying, What man of you, having a hundred sheep, if he lose one of them, doth not leave the ninety and nine in the wilderness, and go after that which is lost, until he find it? And when he hath found it, he layeth it on his shoulders, rejoicing. And when he cometh home, he calleth together his friends and neighbours, saying unto them, Rejoice with me; for I have found my sheep which was lost. I say unto you, that likewise joy shall be in heaven over one sinner that repenteth, more than over ninety and nine just persons, which need no repentance.

> Either what woman having ten pieces of silver, if she lose one piece, doth not light a candle, and sweep the house, and seek diligently till she find it? And when she hath found it, she calleth her friends and her neighbours together, saying, Rejoice with me; for I have found the piece which I had lost. Likewise, I say unto you, there

is joy in the presence of the angels of God over one sinner that repenteth. And he said, A certain man had two sons: And the younger of them said to his father, Father, give me the portion of goods that falleth to me. And he divided unto them his living. And not many days after the younger son gathered all together, and took his journey into a far country, and there wasted his substance with riotous living. And when he had spent all, there arose a mighty famine in that land; and he began to be in want. And he went and joined himself to a citizen of that country; and he sent him into his fields to feed swine. And he would fain have filled his belly with the husks that the swine did eat: and no man gave unto him. And when he came to himself, he said, How many hired servants of my father's have bread enough and to spare, and I perish with hunger! I will arise and go to my father, and will say unto him, Father, I have sinned against heaven, and before thee, And am no more worthy to be called thy son: make me as one of thy hired servants. And he arose, and came to his father. But when he was yet a great way off, his father saw him, and had compassion, and ran, and fell on his neck, and kissed him.

And the son said unto him, Father, I have sinned against heaven, and in thy sight, and am no more worthy to be called thy son. But the father said to his servants, Bring forth the best robe, and put it on him; and put a ring on his hand, and shoes on his feet: And bring hither the fatted calf, and kill it; and let us eat, and be merry: For this my son was dead, and is alive again; he was lost, and is found. And they began to be merry. Now his elder son was in the field: and as he came and drew nigh to the house, he heard music and dancing. And he called one of the servants, and asked what these things meant.

And he said unto him, Thy brother is come; and thy father hath killed the fatted calf, because he hath received him safe and sound. And he was angry, and would not go in: therefore came his father out, and intreated him. And he answering said to his father, Lo, these many years do I serve thee, neither transgressed I at any time thy commandment: and yet thou never gavest me a kid, that I might make merry with my friends: But as soon as this thy son was come, which hath devoured thy living with harlots, thou hast killed for him the fatted calf.

And he said unto him, Son, thou art ever with me, and all that I have is thine. It was meet that we should make merry, and be glad: for this thy brother was dead, and is alive again; and was lost, and is found. (Luke 15:1–32)

One final note on what fishing for souls looks and sounds like. It is the conversation by observation. If the one being fished for does not initiate the conversation, it is wise for the fisherman of souls to use personal observations to initiate a conversation in efforts to win the individual to Christ. Again, since fish are always biting whether in town or out of town, we must always fish. Therefore, on every encounter with people, the fisherman must keenly observe, always looking for en route conversations. These en routes could be commenting on logos on baseball caps, commenting on writing on shirts, commenting on a certain way clothing is worn, commenting on an accent in one's speech, questioning one's hometown, offering to be of assistance with luggage, going out of the way to be kind, approaching and enthusiastically speaking to others, finding common ground, and giving compliments. These are just a start. They open the door to conversation and have proven to lead to something greater later.

There is one more important point to consider. Conversation by observation works the other way as well. Fishermen for souls should bait themselves with appealing clothing, caps, and the like in efforts to cause others to comment or inquire. It's like fishing for bass fish. Bass bite on lures that are shiny, glittery, or sparkly. In other words, that which is attractive gets the attention of bass. This works with people as well. People are attracted to what is attractive for attractiveness arouses their curiosity, which could lead to conversation, communication, and eventually an opportunity for salvation. I shall never forget the curiosity that was raised in me the day that I spotted a fancy barbecue pit made out of metal that had been molded into the shape of a pistol mounted on a trailer hitched to a truck. I had never seen a rig like that and imagined myself having one. I thought how neat it would be to have one. Seeing that pit gave me a desire to smoke meat. I imagined the meat sitting in the upper part of the bullet chamber and the smoke coming out of the barrel. In an instant—within seconds—as I drove past the pit at sixty miles per hour, I not only desired that pit but was willing to turn my car around and entertain conversation with the owner about it. Fishermen must make themselves attractive and appealing to others because just like the bass, if they like what they see, they will take the bait.

14

Hold Your Mouth Right

When I was a little boy and would struggle with catching fish, my dad would always say, "You are not catching fish because you are not holding your mouth right."

That puzzled me for years. I really thought that I did put my mouth in the right position, so I tried positioning and repositioning it in all types of ways. But it never worked. I had an idea that there was more to it than that, and when I grew older, I realized that my dad really was not talking about my mouth. He was talking about my attitude. Having the right attitude about fishing is extremely important.

One aspect of having the right attitude is determination. Fishing is not easy. It takes determination to wake up early, find the proper bait, seek out and drive to the body of water, wade through grass if fishing on land or launch a boat if fishing in a boat, catch the fish, and clean the fish.

The same determination is required when fishing for souls. Those who fish for men must be willing to do whatever necessary to save souls. When setting out to fish for fish or for souls, there is no guarantee of a catch. But that is the risk the determined are willingly to take. The unknown does not move or alter the determined fisherman's plans to catch fish. He is determined and always prepared to make it happen despite the obstacles. What fish are to the fisher of fish are what lost souls are to the fisher of men.

Another aspect of having the right attitude is positive thinking. Every true fisherman must think positively and have a mind-over-matter attitude. On any given fishing trip, anything and everything could go wrong. For example, bad weather and fish that will not bite. But the fisherman with the right attitude exercises patience, encourages himself, and exhausts every effort to catch fish.

Fishing for souls also requires positive thinking. It is one of the most rewarding and difficult things a believer will ever do. For one's own edification, believers must remember how difficult the conversion process was for them and allow that to guide and guard their thinking. Displaying positive thinking requires patience and a relentless determination to see a soul saved. For the soul winner, quitting is never an option. The soul winner is willing to go above and beyond to get positive results.

Fishing by Faith and Works

Fishing for fish requires faith. But faith alone will not help. James said that faith without works is dead (James 2:20). Faith alone will not bring fish out of the water. Therefore, by faith and on a daily basis, believers should bait the hook, cast the bait, and wait for something to happen.

Fishing for souls is a faith movement that also requires work. There is no way to win souls without doing something. Jesus must be placed on display in the life of the believer, so unbelievers can see that Jesus is clearly evident in the believer's life. It must be remembered that fish don't jump into boats. Fish do not give themselves up. Every fish caught is the result of a fish sought. If there is no seeking, there is no reaping.

Catching fish and catching souls require faith and works. Fishing with faith but without works in a fisherman's life is fruitless and unrewarding, and it gives a fish another day to live. However, fishing with faith and works is fruitful and rewarding and will save a soul from death.

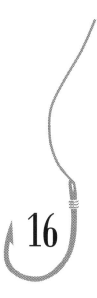

The Big Mystery

There is no way to determine what will be caught after casting bait into the water. Therefore, the mystery of each cast's results should be approached with great excitement and expectations.

Witnessing to unbelievers is no different. One will never know what's inside people. Wouldn't it be great if people wore their spiritual gifts on the outside? But that's not the case. What's inside people is revealed once they come out of sin and into Christ. For this cause, we must do the legwork as fishers of men to get unbelievers to Christ so that the great mystery of who they really are is made known to the church and world. When I came to Christ, Carolyn Softly had no idea that she was witnessing to a man who would two years later mysteriously announce a call to preach the gospel, and within sixteen years, become the founding pastor of one church in three locations in three cities. Fishing for lost souls unveils and reveals the mysteries of life.

17

The Calculated Caster

A fisherman must first know how to cast the line. Much practice should be dedicated to this skill before moving to the water to fish. (By the way, there is a reel made specifically for lefthanded fishermen.) Practice can take place in a yard, an open field, or even a grocery store parking lot. The more skilled the fisherman is with casting, the more successful he or she will be at the water. The fisherman must be able to place the bait in a desired place. This increases the chances of catching fish.

Precision casting is important. For instance, certain fish, such as gasper goo (also known as the freshwater drum), commonly bite in running water where the current creates a swirl in the water. Therefore, it is highly recommended to cast the line in the running water in the swirl. If the fisherman cannot successfully cast the line there, chances of catching fish will inevitably diminish.

Fishermen must highly consider the cast and be calculated casters for there is much riding on each cast. An off-target cast that misses the mark could be fruitless and aggravating. Furthermore, there is nothing worse than knowing where the fish are and not being able to cast the line in their direction.

Fishermen of souls must be calculated casters as well. As fishermen of souls, there must be a deliberate and accurate seeking of lost men's souls that occurs before reaching the witnessing destination. In other words, the necessary homework is completed, and there is prior knowledge of where to go, what to do, and what to say before the fisherman gets where he or she is going. This fisherman knows what to do and what to say at the grocery store, football game, basketball game, and dance recital in order to get good results. For example, if at a football game, the wise fisher of souls is advised to cast the bait (Jesus) in the parking lot after a game, especially after a loss, rather than during a game while in the bleachers. Down and hopeless moments and other teachable and soul-thirsting moments constitute good places to cast witnessing for Jesus. Fishermen, make every cast count!

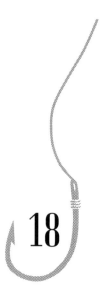

18

Don't Take the Bite for Granted

A bite on the line should never be taken for granted. It should be handled with the utmost care, consideration, and gratefulness.

There are times when the only thing that will be caught is a suntan or even a cold. Catching fish is not easy or guaranteed, and it should not be taken for granted. When a fish gives the bait interest, it is more than just a bite; it is the favor of God. It is actually food on the table. So many people regularly spend countless hours on the pond only to leave disappointed and empty, having not entertained a single bite. This gives great evidence for why those who catch fish should be grateful.

When a nonbeliever shows interest in God or the things of God, special care and concern must be shown to that individual. Believers must not distract or handle that person nonchalantly. Nonbelievers usually feel justified in their ungodly lifestyles and are usually unreceptive to anything new, strange, or uncommon to them—such as the gospel. Therefore, interest in the gospel must be nurtured until the nonbeliever is safely landed or connected to the body of Christ and rooted in the gospel. The believer must understand this is a rare occurrence that should not be taken for granted. Rather, it should be taken advantage of.

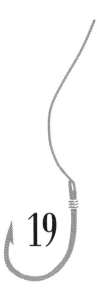

19

Applying the Drag

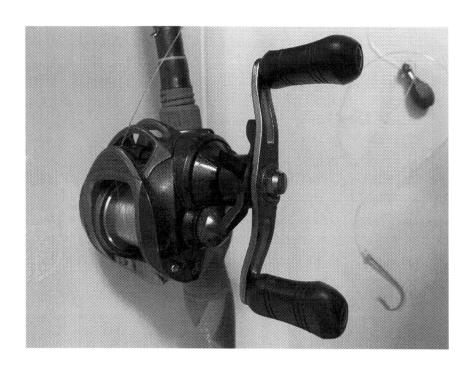

Setting the hook in the fish's mouth is one thing, but getting the fish securely out of the water is another. There is nothing more heartbreaking than to set the hook in the fish's mouth, reel the fish in part of the way, and then lose it.

Sometimes big fish, if not handled properly, break the line or take the hook off the line. This usually happens when the fisherman uses inadequate line or fails to use a feature located on the reel called the drag. The drag is a little turn wheel that adjusts the tension of the line. If the drag is tightened, the line is locked in a tight position, creating a tension against the fish. If the line is rated for fish weighing twenty pounds and the catch is thirty pounds, with a tightened line and no drag, there is a good chance the fish will break the line or take the hook.

However, if the drag is on, the wheel in the loosened position allows the fish to take additional line, easing the tension on the reel and prevent the line from breaking. It also prevents the fish from taking the hook. In this case, a ten-pound test line with proper drag could successfully withstand the weight of a twenty-pound fish.

Many good fish have been lost due to poor fishing practices. The drag could have helped so many fishers for fish, but failure to use the drag caused them to come up empty. The entire intent of the drag is to give the fish an opportunity to wear itself out. Fish will not give in easily. They will put up a fight that will last for what seems like an eternity, but the drag is the fisherman's friend. Once the fish gives up the fight, it comes in with ease. The drag literally takes the fight out of the fish.

People are the same way. Using the drag could have helped fishers of souls as well. Once people are hooked, it may take a while to get them out of their elements or environments. The sinners' struggles with change pose an issue for the fisherman, so the fisherman must use the drag, giving the individuals the space they need while keeping the tension as they are reeled in to safety. Sinners should not be forced into anything. The believer must maintain a constant presence in the sinner's life while allowing them the freedom needed to entertain, process, and embrace change. While the sinner is on the line, never lose sight of the fact that it does not matter how far they wander; while on the drag, they are still caught and carrying the hook of salvation in their mouths. It is usually just a matter of time before they are worn out, fully landed, and connected to ministry.

You Catch Some and You Miss Some ... Just Keep Fishing

It does not matter how skilled a fisherman is or how long a fisherman has been in the sport; a fisherman will catch some, and he or she will miss some. The goal is to keep fishing because there is more to be thankful for than to be discouraged about. The faithful fishermen will catch far more fish than they will miss—if they keep fishing.

I must admit that missing fish leaves an empty spot in the pit of the stomach, especially if the fish was a big one. The feeling of missing a fish is indescribably upsetting, but amid the miss, another possibly bigger fish awaits the opportunity to bite. Therefore, let it go, bait the hook, cast the line, and get ready for the next fish.

When fishing for souls, there will be moments of disappointment as those who showed so much interest and seemed so promising suddenly move on. Many people live in guilt, faulting themselves and not realizing that some things are out of their control. It is far better to have entertained a fish on the line than to have not had a bite at all. If the faithful fisherman did all that could be done to ensure a catch but suffered a loss, that fish was not meant to be caught by that fisherman. Just keep fishing! There are countless fish of all types and sizes in the water, all waiting on opportunities at the bait. Keep fishing. Fishing for lost souls requires the same mindset. As they say, "Don't cry over spilled milk." Just move on and see what the sea of uncertainly will offer next. The fisherman will never know what lies ahead unless he or she keeps fishing.

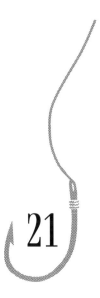

Feeding Is Seeding

A missed opportunity to catch a fish is never a loss. The least that was done was the feeding of the fish. Feeding is seeding and futuristically benefits the fish, the next potential fisherman, and the seeder. Here is more good news for the seeder. Galatians 6:7 says, "Be not deceived; God is not mocked: for whatsoever a man soweth, that shall he also reap." As the psalmist says in Psalm 30:5, "weeping may endure for a night but joy cometh in the morning." And Psalm 126:5, 6 says, "They that sow in tears shall reap in joy. He that goeth forth and weepeth, bearing precious seed, shall doubtless come again with rejoicing, bringing his sheaves with him." Missing a few must be viewed differently for weeping will one day turn into reaping due to the biblical principle of sowing and reaping. The feeder should rejoice when missing a fish. As the apostle Paul said, "And let us not be weary in well doing: for in due season we shall reap, if we faint not." (Galatians 6:9).

When fishing for souls, one must always bear in mind what the apostle Paul said in 1 Corinthians 3:6–10:

> I have planted, Apollos watered; but God gave the
> increase. So then neither is he that planteth any thing,

neither he that watereth; but God that giveth the increase. Now he that planteth and he that watereth are one: and every man shall receive his own reward according to his own labour. For we are labourers together with God: ye are God's husbandry, ye are God's building. According to the grace of God which is given unto me, as a wise master-builder, I have laid the foundation, and another buildeth thereon. But let every man take heed how he buildeth thereupon.

We must understand that we play a huge part in the redemptive process of others as we work along with God. This means that as long as fishers of souls are fishing, whether we gain catch or lose them, as long as we are fishing, we are still making a difference for the kingdom of God.

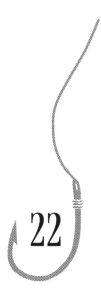

Twenty-First-Century Fishing Concerns

Here we are in November, in the year 2020 of our Lord, and I am amazed at how people don't fish or have never had a fishing experience. It is interesting to note that most of Jesus's disciples were fishermen. But this does not come as a surprise, considering the fact that fishing for actual fish is no different than fishing for lost men's and women's souls. Could it be that the devil, in his scheme to secure souls for himself, has made it his business to keep men and fathers out of their young boys' lives in an effort to keep them away from the fish pond? Could it further be the concern of the devil that Jesus might call these young boys from the fish pond as He did the first disciples, who later fished for men and turned the world right side up? Could it be that the devil for fear of losing souls to his kingdom has busied up man to the point that man does not have time to fish, much less time to take someone else fishing? How tragic considering Christianity had its humble beginnings through the faithful hands of real fishermen and that its continued success has been aided by the faithful hands of past and current fishermen of souls.

Fishing to some extent is in every individual. COVID-19 has proven that to be true as it has revealed the fisherman in many people in this pandemic season. The shelves of major sporting goods stores and especially Walmart super stores were completely void of most of their fishing gear stock when people were faced with having more time on their hands. More quarantined individuals turned to fishing than to any other outdoor activity. It is because fishing is embedded deeply within every soul, not so much to catch fish, but to catch souls. Unbeknown to the individual, fishing for souls is really a dormant desire that is fleshed out through fishing for fish.

Fishing is in everybody, even children. Most young boys enjoy fishing from their first encounter. Even young girls enjoy it the same. Most children who fish as children will one day between childhood and the grave revisit the sport.

My heart went out to two women, who both appeared to be in their thirties, and one teenage girl as they all sought to fish using the tight-line method. One had experience, which she more than likely gained from her father as a child. The other woman had little experience and made little progress as she followed the lead of the other woman. The teenage girl, bless her heart, did not have any experience at all and spent most of her time in confusion, fear, timidity, disgust, and disconnect. It was a horrible but admirable scene to watch. It was horrible in the sense that they were not going to put any food on the table from those waters. It was admirable in the sense that at least they were trying. I stood not far from them sorrowfully, thinking, *What a difference a man could have made in those women's lives*. This could have been a different scene if a man with fishing experience had been there, or if some man had previously taken the time to thoroughly teach the art of fishing. Ed Bruce was sending out a message to his listening audience when in 1975 he said these words in the title of his classic country song, "Mammas, Don't Let Your Babies Grow Up to Be Cowboys." I cannot say much to that. But I can say that mammas ought to let their babies grow up to be fishermen so that when Jesus saves them, they will be knowledgeable and ready to fish for souls.

Then there is a view that can be contributed to common fact the old saying, "Give a man a fish, and he'll beg for a fish for the rest of his life. Teach a man to fish, and he will feed himself for the rest of his life." How true! How true! How true! The first part of this saying is painfully actualized in the world today. Therefore, the second part should be the prayer and task of all to provide hope to a world that is suffering from physical and spiritual starvation, and to a world that is in a constant state of survival.

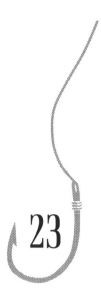

23

The Joy of Catching Fish

Catching a fish has to be among the top five most exhilarating moments in life. It is the result, reward, and climax of all the money, preparation, faith, and patience invested.

The fishing experience can be described in three exciting and thrilling integrated parts. First, there is the bite. Then comes setting the hook in the fish's mouth and the bending of the pole. Next comes the feeling of reeling in the fish, which is the first of the integrated parts.

The second of the integrated parts is the moment that unveils the great mystery concerning the type and size of the fish on the line. There is something unique and intriguing about the first face-to-face encounter with the catch. There is a sensational feeling associated with this unveiling moment that builds a sense of pride and ownership within the fisherman. Others live to see the catch, but the fisherman lives to show off the catch.

The last of the integrated parts is to see how in an instant nothing becomes something and how empty becomes full. This leads to the grand finale and great transition as the event shifts mentally and physically from not just catching a fish but to enjoying a delicious fish meal at the table with family and friends.

The joy of catching fish is wrapped up in this: "It's not solely about what the fish present once pulled out of the water that's most important but rather, what the fish shall be that matters most." What a joy!

The previous paragraphs are the exact description of what it feels like to fish for and catch a soul. The integrated parts excitingly apply to each fishing experience and yield great joy and awesome rewards. They should inspire all believers to want to become fishers of men. I have had the opportunity to see many people, especially women, catch their first fish, and it blessed me every time. It blesses me because the entire experience has continually proven to be life-changing and more desired by each one who had the experience. To top it off, the entire experience is literally a setup for a rise in an unbeliever's life that leaves all parties involved better.

Though many first-time fish catchers have not yet made the transition to fishing for souls, prayerfully they will. I believe this book will serve its purpose of helping fishers of men to make the connection while seeing the correlation between fishing for fish and fishing for men. I truly believe that when these fishers of men get the revelation from the correlation, all parties involved will never be the same. Church, the best is yet to come!

24

Catch-'Em, and Then What?

Fish were meant to be caught, cleaned, and enjoyed. Failure to do so is foolishness to the one who denies and rejects them and mockery to the Creator who made them and gave them to the world. Fish have major nutritional value that affects many aspects of the human body. Though there are those who are allergic to seafood, fish is one of the main and most popular foods consumed by human beings.

This information should not come as a surprise to anyone considering that in the beginning, God sent forth the water and shortly thereafter created the fish, both small and great, to occupy those waters. Then not many days later, God created man and gave him dominion over them all and the authority to eat of the life that He created, fish included (Genesis 1). This was God's doing, and it should be marvelous in man's sight.

There have been times when I caught fish that were really too small to bring home, but I did not realize it until I got home. Many small fish that I should have returned to the water have died in my care. To pacify my guilt, I found no other choice but to return those fish to the water in their dead state so that at least a predator, such as an alligator, would have a meal. Rather than tossing those fish into the trash can and letting them become waste, I have on many occasions driven two miles or more to release those fish into the water so that their purpose for being a fish would be properly served. Fish have a purpose that must be fulfilled. It is the responsibility of those bearing dominion and authority to see that the fish entrusted to their care serve their God-intended purpose.

When souls have been caught by the gospel fisherman, it is the responsibility of the fisherman to facilitate the next move for that individual's life. Many new converts have seen the trash can because of poor judgment and neglect at the hands of the careless fisherman. This is so unfortunate, but it happens every day. Each soul we catch, whether large or small, has a divine purpose. It is the fisherman's responsibility to help them to fulfill that purpose. When a fish exits the water, that helpless and hopeless fish's next move becomes totally dependent on the fisherman. That soul removed from the world is dependent on the one who did the removing. It is best not to fish at all than to catch fish and let them die.

Strict precautions should be taken and great care undertaken regarding the catch. When fish are caught, they must be immediately and properly secured on ice in buckets or an ice chest. The purpose is to keep them fresh and free of predators such as flies, snakes, alligators, and cats. Fishermen are not the only creatures that like fish. Predators will prey on the catch for their own selfish good. Therefore, the catch must be guarded.

I remember a fishing occasion when I decided to use a metal fish stringer to hold and keep my fish alive and fresh while dangling in the waters of their natural habitat while I continued to fish. Much to my surprise, when it was time to leave, I pulled the metal stringer out of the water and discovered that water moccasins had already begun feasting on my catch.

Furthermore, when fish are caught, it is important to enjoy them. not let them sit in the freezer for a long period. Fish that sit in the freezer too long can become freezer burned, which drastically alters the taste of the fish.

It is highly recommended that new converts immediately go through a discipleship program of the church, become tested for spiritual gifts, and placed in ministry to avoid damage caused by Christian inactivity.

25

The Dirty Work

People are like fish. They must be cleaned before they can be used.

For a long time the part I dreaded most about fishing was, and I say "was," cleaning the fish. This entailed scraping the scales from the fish or skinning the catfish, followed by chopping off the head and removing the entrails. During the process of removing the entrails, the repulsive smell literally takes one's breath away. The process is always the same each time fish are caught, and one never gets immune to the smell.

But the Lord brought about

a change, and now I no longer dread cleaning the fish. It took having a bigger purpose in mind for the fish I caught to change my attitude about cleaning them. I developed a fish wish list at the church that entailed giving the fish away after being cleaned and washed. Whoever wanted fish simply indicated it on a form I devised, and within weeks, I honored the list. Most of the list consisted of widows and the elderly, and I could not justify them cleaning their own fish. So I decided to clean their fish for them. Interestingly, I struggled with cleaning fish for my own table, but when I began to do it for others, my entire attitude changed. That which I dreaded has now become the highlight of each trip. The fish has a higher purpose and a better purpose, which has brought a delight in the cleaning process, thus removing all the dread.

The church has been known to score relatively low in the area of cleaning the fish, which is teaching and discipling new converts. The church rejoices to see them come through the doors and join the church but struggles with the next crucial step of cleaning them up. When the church of the living God gets to the point where it does not mind doing the dirty work, incoming believers will become more solid in the scriptures, mature in their Christian walks, and better-equipped for the work of the ministry. Then the church will grow by leaps and bounds.

26

Getting Practical

Fishing Success Progression Steps

Prior to a trip, plan a fishing trip. Choose the date; choose the place and time of departure. Prepare and pack the gear, which includes ice chest, fishing pole, tackle box, bait, and other necessities.

Once the destination is reached, cast the line and wait on a bite. When fish are caught, clean them, prepare them for cooking, cook them, and enjoy them. (The more the merrier.) The fish would have then served their God-intended purpose.

Evangelical Success Progression Steps

When fishing for souls, the same process applies. Plan an evangelism trip; choose the date, place, and time. Prepare those items needed for the trip, such as the Bible, witnessing tracts, and business cards.

Once the destination is reached, begin the process of fishing for the souls by utilizing your soul-winning tools—the tracts. When the souls are caught, personally or through the local church, disciple (clean) them, expose them to spiritual gifts test (cooking), and finally, enjoy the new creature in Christ as they now serve their God-intended purposes.

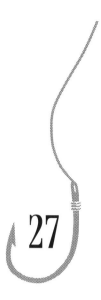

The Result of All the Effort

The result of all the effort put forth in fishing for souls is ultimately to please God while exposing the kingdom of God to all creatures He created in His image and likeness so that they might experience His unconditional love through salvation. Therefore, it should be the responsibility of every believer who has experienced God and is the product of another man's fishing experience to be obedient to the Great Commission, to be obsessed with a desire to be like Christ, and to be overjoyed to see sinners experience change.

The infallible Word of God has preeminence over all things. It should always be the guide and instruction manual for all believers to follow. What the Lord commands in His Word, the believer, out of obedience to the Lord's Word and will, must do. Matthew 28:18–20 is not an exception. Jesus, prior to His ascension to be with the Father, left believing disciples who would form the church a direct command:

> And Jesus came and spake unto them, saying, All power is given unto me in heaven and in earth. Go ye therefore, and teach all nations, baptizing them in the name of the Father, and of the Son, and of the Holy Ghost:

Teaching them to observe all things whatsoever I have commanded you: and, lo, I am with you alway, even unto the end of the world. Amen.

Plainly stated, Jesus was saying, "Go fishing." Jesus did not ask the disciples to go. Nor did He desire a conference to discuss the matter. He did not put the matter up for a vote. He simply commanded them to go. As found in Acts chapter 2, at the time of Pentecost, the disciples, out of obedience, went, and lives changed drastically as the commission was obeyed. It seems as though the farther the world gets from Calvary's hill, where Jesus died on a cross and the grave from which Jesus rose, the more insignificant and obsolete the commission has become to the church and believers. If this sinful world will experience any change for the better, it will happen only if believers once again obediently embrace and carry out this great command of Jesus Christ with all seriousness and dedication.

Additionally, every believer must become obsessed with a desire to be like Christ. Being like Christ entails doing all things in the manner in which He would do them. Furthermore, being Christlike is the actual seeking to live the Word of God to the best of one's ability. It is making the Word of God top priority. Being like Christ is a concentrated effort on behalf of the believer to commit to Jesus's teachings and pattern of living to the point of obsession. When this lifestyle becomes an obsession, the believer will then imitate Jesus Christ and influence lives with the gospel while displaying a fisherman's mentality everywhere he or she goes and at all times of the day. Fishing for souls was natural and an obsession for Jesus Christ because He bore the agenda of the Father. Saints of God, we, too, must bear the agenda of God through Jesus Christ, and in time, our evangelistic behaviors will influence lives in the manner in which Jesus did when He walked on the earth.

Finally, believers do what they do as fishermen because they know the reality of change and the reality of being set free. The joy that the believer possesses has no limits. The freedom that the believer possesses has no boundaries. The love that the believer possesses has no depths. The true believer has this great treasure and desires for all men and woman to have this same joy, liberty, love, and eventually eternal life. Therefore, the believer who fishes for souls is always overjoyed to see changes in the lives of sinners for he or she realizes that fishing for souls is the responsibility of every believer.

The Tackle Box

Every fisherman should always own and bring a tackle box filled with everything needed to ensure a successful fishing trip. The tackle box is usually stocked with hooks, weights, line, lures, pliers, slicker suit, important papers, and much more.

I have concluded this book with some much-needed tackle the fisherman will need to be successful when fishing for fish and for souls. The tackle exists in the form of fishing truths, fish and fishing facts, tips and wisdom, reminders and recommendations, and benefits.

Fishing Truths

> For he was astonished, and all that were with him, at the draught of the fishes which they had taken: And so was also James, and John, the sons of Zebedee, which were partners with Simon. And Jesus said unto Simon, Fear not; from henceforth thou shalt catch men. And when they had brought their ships to land, they forsook all, and followed him. (Luke 5:9–11)

The fruit of the righteous is a tree of life; and he that winneth souls is wise. (Proverbs 11:30)

A true witness delivereth souls: but a deceitful witness speaketh lies. (Proverbs 14:25)

And the lord said unto the servant, Go out into the highways and hedges, and compel them to come in, that my house may be filled. (Luke 14:23)

Fish and Fishing Facts

- Fish can smell.
- Fish can see.
- Fish have incredible instincts and can maneuver quickly in the water.
- Fish bite early in the morning.
- Fish do not bite as well in the middle of the day.
- Fish bite late at night.
- Most people like or eat fish.
- Most people have never been fishing; therefore, they don't know how to fish.
- Younger or smaller fish are considered tender fish, and are generally more enjoyable to eat. Older or larger fish tend to have tougher meat, and some have worms. Furthermore, older or larger fish are harder to clean.
- Fish is one of the few dishes that is prepared and served whole. Yes, you can eat nearly the whole thing.
- Eating hot fish is far better than eating cold fish.
- Fish is known to keep people healthy and alive. Fish oil has omega 3, which is good for the human body.
- Fresh fish is always better than store-bought packed and sealed fish.
- When fishing, you may not catch what you want, and the fish you catch might taste slightly different. But for the most part, all fish taste the same.

Tips and Wisdom

- Gasper goos like freshwater and dead or live bait, such as shrimp, crawfish, and worms. They hang out in running water and still water near the bottom of the water, but they will also bite on the surface of the water. Please note that goos bite better in running water.

- Catfish like fresh bait and hang out in running water and still water. They usually hang out near the bottom of the water, though they will bite on the surface of the water as well. They feed on live or dead shrimp, crawfish, worms, and small fish such as shads and shiners.

- Perch and brim hang out in freshwater near the bank around trees and near foliage in shallow water. They feed on live or dead water insects and small shrimp, as well as small artificial bait. Using a cork or stopper is advised. Setting the cork or stopper two to two and a half feet from the bait is recommended.

- Bass hang out in freshwater near the bank around trees and near foliage in shallow water. They feed on live or dead water insects and artificial bait.

- What do you do when you set the hook properly and the fish is coming in, but then suddenly the fish takes the hook? The fish moved on, so you must move on as well. The fish will bite again, so fish again. However, chances are slim that you will get an opportunity at the same fish you missed. Obviously God did not intend for you to catch that fish. On a higher note, there are bigger fish to be caught than the one you missed.

- It should be the goal of every fisherman to catch big fish. However, be grateful for whatever you catch, and thank God for it. But the ultimate goal should be to catch big fish. Some fish will be enough to feed one person. Some fish will be enough to feed two people. Some fish will be enough to feed a large family. Some fish are able to feed the multitude. Why not get the most for your bait and feed the multitude? Fishermen should always think big and fish for the big ones.

- Applying this to the church, some people will serve and service one or two people well in their lifetimes. Then there are others who will serve a few families well in service onto the Lord in their lifetimes. But then there are others who will serve the multitude, and their names will go down in history as being blessings to many people in many places through many means. Fishermen for souls should always be grateful for the catch but always think big and fish for big fish.

- Some big fish are considered trophies on the wall. In other words, some fishermen will take the big fish and mount it on the main wall in the house for others to see.
- In the church a big fish is known as that individual who accepts Jesus Christ and becomes a mature, seasoned, and a contributing member of a church, making a major difference in every way and impacting many lives.
- Getting snagged or caught up is a part of fishing and should be expected. Getting snagged is when the hook gets stuck on something at the bottom of the water. The best thing to do is break the line by pulling it until the line pops. Then replace the hook and weight.
- Fishing with trotlines and jugs is a good way to catch fish, but it removes the adventure of fishing, the personalization of fishing, and the rewards of fishing.
- Expect a fight when you catch a fish. Fish will always put up a fight when pulled out of their natural environment. This also applies to souls. People will fight and put up great resistance when coming up out of sin. Like fish, people resist coming out of sin, resisting a new and best life in Christ. People commonly resist their God-intended purpose for living.
- Fishermen have been known to stretch the truth, which is to tell a lie. Fishermen of souls must be mindful to always tell the truth … the whole truth and nothing but the truth. The truth makes Jesus (the bait) more attractive and desirable to sinners, and if received, the truth will make sinners free.
- A few fish are called a fry; several fish are called a mess; but many fish are called a draught. Jesus gave Peter a draught in Luke 5, and it forever changed his life and the lives of others to this day. The best way to avoid a "mess" in the church is to catch a draught.

- Wade fishing entails a fisherman actually walking into the water and standing in the very environment where the fish are located. Special water boots are usually worn as the fisherman walks out into shallow water to fish, thus increasing the possibility to catch fish.

  Applied to fishing for souls, the actual going where lost souls are, in the very environment, can make a tremendous difference when seeking to win souls to Jesus Christ.

- During Old Testament times and even today, people fish using cast nets. Cast nets are large, weighted, circular nets designed to capture many fish of various types with each cast. The wider the net spreads, the increased possibility of catching fish. A skillful caster makes a tremendous difference.

  Having church revivals is like fishing with a cast net. It takes a lot of effort, but the potential to gain new prospects for Christ is unlimited. The longer the revival (the wider the net), the increased possibility of winning souls to Christ. A skillful revivalist makes a tremendous difference.

- Church signs and bulletin boards have luring power when used appropriately. People read signs; it is a natural instinct. Therefore, church signs and bulletin boards should always be kept attractive and current. God will use a sign or a bulletin board to draw people to Himself.

Reminders and Recommendations

- Place a limit on the food you bring to the fishing pond. Overeating could quench your hunger for catching fish.
- Using the right hook makes a big difference for tight-line fishing.
- Using the right sinker is important for tight-line fishing.
- Using the right test line makes a difference.
- Always bring a net.
- Always keep the bait fresh.
- Always have plenty of tackle on hand.
- Always have mosquito spray.
- Always have clothing conducive to the weather, including a rain suit.

- Always have sunglasses and sunscreen.

Benefits

- Fishing is refreshing and relaxing.
- Fishing is an excellent place to meditate.
- Fishing supplies food for the table.
- Fishing will keep your fishing for souls skills sharp and visa versa.
- Fishing could be a blessing to others. One person's pleasure could become someone else's dinner.

Testimonials

Logan Fields

L ogan Fields, my sixteen-year-old nephew and neighbor, had never been fishing, so he had never caught a fish. All of that changed on April 1, 2020, as Logan shared a fishing experience with me on the banks of a Verdunville canal.

Logan had this to say concerning his experience:

> The feeling of catching my first fish was exhilarating. It was very thrilling to pull the fish out the water, and in that moment, fishing taught me to never take anything for granted. You have to enjoy the little things in life, even if it's just catching a fish or talking with someone because you never know when it could be the last time.

Mark and Swanzetta Joseph

Brother Mark Joseph and Sister Swanzetta Joseph, faithful members of the Lighthouse, both had their first fishing experience with First Lady Randle and me on July 31, 2020.

Brother Mark Joseph, LMBC facility coordinator, had this to say:

> I have fished before in the past, but my latest fishing experiences have been the most joyful and memorable experiences.

My first experience on a boat was with Pastor Randle. I was a little nervous at first, but after a while, I got comfortable. I had to get brave really fast since we were talking about bringing our wives with us one day.

A few weeks later, my wife and the first lady joined us on the boat. It was then that I fell in love with fishing. It is now a must do. My wife and I go fishing together at least once a week, but she goes alone almost every day since she learned how to do everything on her own.

The one thing that I value most from all these fishing trips is the quality time I get to spend with my wife. We get to laugh, talk, and enjoy each other more.

Whether on the boat or on land, fishing is very calming and peaceful.

Sister Swanzetta Joseph, LMBC youth director, had this to say:

My first fishing experience was absolutely the most amazing outdoor experience that I have ever had. In the beginning I was a little apprehensive about the boat ride. Being that close to that much water was not something on my bucket list. However, I thought it would be a fun experience.

Moments after the boat took off I became scared for a moment, but as I looked around; everyone else was calm and enjoying the ride, so I began to loosen up a little. As we got further out into the bayou, the scenery became even more beautiful from where we began. The sky was a beautiful blue, and you could see the sunrise from a distance between the trees as the reflection of the sun appeared upon the water. This was just a beautiful sight. I immediately began reflecting on Genesis 1 and God's creation of all these wonderful things.

After finding a location to dock our boat, my husband fixed up my line and cast it into the water. We did not get much action in that spot, so we moved around to another location. At that point I became anxious because my husband, Pastor Randle, and the first lady had already caught at least one fish. I was ready to catch one too. My husband whispered something to me that is very important when fishing. He said, "Bae, you have to be patient. It will come to you. just be patient." Well I did just that. He cast my line the second time and the third time, and then finally, something pulled on my line. My first catch! Now I will not exaggerate like most fishermen when it comes down to what they catch, but I do believe my first catch had to be about fifteen to twenty pounds.

And this happened because I had just a little patience. I waited patiently on the bite, and I eventually caught a fish.

This also applies to being fishermen of men. Being a fishermen of men is very similar to fishing. If you want to lead others to Christ, then you must have patience.

You must talk about the Word of God wherever you go with hopes of reaching those who do not know Christ. Once you cast out the Word, it is very important to be patient while waiting so that you do not miss the catch. Jesus was patient while He was waiting on us, so we must be patient while waiting for others. Then finally, once you catch them, do not leave their side. Just as Jesus never left us, stay close to them, and help them to become a strong and mature Christian so that they can later become fishermen of men too.

Yardina Wilson

Brother Wilson and Sister Yardina Wilson, faithful members of the Lighthouse, shared a fishing experience with First Lady Randle and me on September 12, 2020.

Brother Wilson is a deacon of the church and had previous fishing experiences. However, Sister Wilson, church greeter, caught her first fish and had this to say:

Wow, what an experience!

This was an experience that I will never forget! I have had many experiences throughout my life—including traveling within the United States and abroad, meeting famous people, dining at some of the finest restaurants, zip-lining, snorkeling, and jet skiing—but fishing on a boat was something I can say I had ever experienced. Being a city girl, fishing in a boat was not on my bucket list until I moved to south Louisiana more than twenty years ago. I had heard from several acquaintances how much fun and how relaxing fishing on a boat was, so I wanted to experience it for myself.

What better way to have that experience than with my pastor, Pastor Allen Ray Randle Sr. and First Lady Pamela Randle. What a trip to remember! So much laughter and being amazed at God's creation as our "Captain," Pastor Randle, maneuvered through the open waterways. I must say he handles his boat pretty well! He was very careful and made sure I was comfortable and not afraid. My father taught me to swim at the age of five, along with my siblings, and we had a members-only neighborhood swimming pool, park, and lake directly behind our home. We could walk right out of our backyard about five feet and arrive at the gates of the pool. That has played a part in my life not being afraid of water.

Once I settled down from the excitement of actually being on a boat and soaking in how amazing God is with His creations, the excitement began. I was very attentive as we matriculated through the waters as Pastor steered his boat!

Captain-pastor stopped the boat, and he and Deacon Wilson put down the anchors. I have always wondered how boats could somehow stay in place while people fish.

Of course Deacon Wilson knew I was not baiting the hook. City girl was not getting her hands dirty; he knew that was his assignment. Although Deacon Wilson had me practice casting the line in the backyard so that I didn't embarrass him, I still was not the best caster. But I was a good enough caster to catch my first fish. Talk about excited! Although it was not a big fish, I was still excited. Goal accomplished.

I was only familiar with catfish, brim, sac-a-lait, and perch. Well I was told I caught a goujon catfish, and I think the first lady caught a gasper goo. To my surprise,

I had never heard of goujon catfish or gasper goo. Let me tell you, the first lady has this fishing thing down to a science. I caught two or three fish during my trip and had several bites.

As we began to bring our trip to an end, I had a huge bite. Unfortunately, I lost what I thought was the shark from *Jaws* due to what is known as "drag adjustment." That brought our trip to an end.

It is my understanding that the pastor-captain went back later in the week and caught my Jaws!

Fishing on a boat with my pastor and first lady was definitely a trip to remember.

Dianne Jones

Pastor Charles Jones and First Lady Diane Jones of New Hope Missionary Baptist Church of Houston, Texas, shared a fishing experience with Pamela and me on November 6, 2020. Pastor Jones had previous experience with fishing and previous encounters with catching fish. Dianne, however, caught her first fish and had this to say:

My first fishing experience was not what I thought it would be. I have been desiring to go fishing for several years. I talked about it and mentioned it to my husband several times. However, he does not know much about fishing, and it never seemed to be the right time and tolerable weather. It is very hot in Houston, Texas, and when it is not very hot, it is very humid with lots of mosquitoes. After several failed attempts, I did what most people over fifty do: I created a bucket list, and going fishing was at the top of the list. As you can probably tell by now, I had very high expectations for my first perfect fishing experience. I shared my desire to go fishing with the Randles, and they were more than happy to help me fulfill my desire. We set a date and started planning our five and a half-hour drive to Franklin, Louisiana. I did not realize at that time that checking the weather is a very important part of planning a fishing trip. Two days before we were scheduled to head to Louisiana, we found out that there was a hurricane headed straight toward Franklin. Unfortunately, I was not to fulfill my desire to go fishing that weekend. I started thinking that maybe fishing was not for me. As I started coming to terms with not going fishing, Pamela contacted me about rescheduling our fishing trip. That interaction with Pamela reignited my desire, and another date was set. A few weeks later, we were entering the city of Franklin and had plans to go fishing early Friday morning. During the ride to Louisiana, I started thinking about my motion sickness and the possibility of getting sick on the boat. I also started thinking about how I would feel if I didn't catch any fish. Well I prayed that I wouldn't get sick, and I just wanted at least one fish to sacrifice its life for me.

The day finally came, and we headed to the lake. Once we got there, I watched the process of getting the boat in the water and planning our route. There were so many details, but everything seemed very seamless for Pastor Randle. We finally started heading to our first fishing spot, and the weather was a little colder than I expected. However, as the sun started to rise, it warmed up, and I thought everything was perfect for me to catch a lot of fish. I was ready but not totally ready for the complete fishing experience. I wanted to catch fish, but I did not want to touch the bait or the fish. Therefore, my husband and Pastor Randle agreed to take care of those two things for me. Praise God.

Pastor Randle found a spot and showed my husband how to drop the anchors. He was glad to have someone helping him with the anchors because they are very heavy. After dropping the anchors, preparing and putting the bait on the hooks, and assigning the fishing rods, my perfect fishing experience began. My husband was the first to catch a fish. I was super-excited to watch him catch it. Pastor Randle and Pamela caught their fish soon after my husband caught his first. Needless to say, I was still patiently waiting. I finally felt something on my line, and I pulled it in with excitement. When I finally got it to the boat, we realized that I had just caught a, what Pastor Randle called a, "fish stick," which is actually just a stick. We laughed and continued fishing.

We eventually moved to different places on the lake to try to find a good spot, and I still hadn't caught a fish. I would pull my line up and find out a fish had eaten part of my bait. Pastor Randle would take it off and put a new one on. He kept reminding my husband and me that presentation is very important and that it is not good to cast your line if the presentation—bait—is not on the hook properly. I found myself gazing at the water and not really paying attention to the nibble of my bait that

I was supposed to be watching for. I was mesmerized by the calming effects of the water and the sounds of nature.

I began to realize that Pastor Randle was more anxious about my catching a fish now than I was. I had basically resigned myself to the fact that today was not the day for me to catch fish, and I was happy with the experience. But Pastor Randle kept encouraging me and teaching me fishing techniques. So to relieve him from feeling bad that I had not caught a fish, I suggested that since he had caught several, why did he not catch the fish and let me reel it in. Without hesitation, he said, "Nope, that will not count as your catch. That would be my catch."

So the fishing continued. After several pep talks, laughs, and silent prayers, I finally caught a fish. I felt a nibble on the line and announced it to everyone in the boat. Everyone stopped what they were doing to help and cheer me on. Pastor Randle, who I now call the fishing expert, watched my line and told me exactly when to pull to hook it in the fish's mouth and when to start reeling it in. It was a great feeling finally to see the results of my efforts. And yes, I only caught one fish. However, my friend Pamela caught her goal of five.

I mentioned at the beginning of this testimony that my first-time fishing experience was not what I thought it would be. It was far more than I thought it would be with a lot of life-applicable situations that I did not expect. I still think about those experiences. Here are a few that have really stuck with me:

• I asked Pastor Randle to take me fishing because he has a boat, has caught many fish, and goes fishing often. *Life Application:* When seeking help, look for someone who has experience and a desire to share it. I should not ask someone who only has experience hunting deer to teach me to catch fish.

- Our original plan to go fishing was cancelled due to the hurricane. *Life Application:* Things will happen in God's timing. Do not be discouraged because He know the plans that He has for my life, and He has already gone before me. God is in control.

- Pastor Randle kept reminding us to put the bait on the hook properly because presentation is important. *Life Application:* Do not half-do anything. Put your best foot forward every time, and strive for excellence.

- My first catch was a "fish stick." *Life Application:* Do not give up if your first try does not work. Stay committed and keep trying to reach your goal. Also, do not give up on your goals when people are not who you expect them to be.

- I asked Pastor Randle to catch the fish and let me reel it in. *Life Application:* Do not take shortcuts, and do not try to take credit for others' efforts. Be true and authentic.

- My goal and prayer was for one fish to sacrifice its life, and that is exactly what I got, one fish. *Life Application:* Be careful when you pray, and do not limit your prayers because of fear or doubt.

- I prayed for one fish. *Life Application:* God answered my exact prayer. He heard my request and gave me the desire of my heart.

- Pamela's goal every time she goes fishing is to catch at least five fish. *Life Application:* Have friends who will inspire you to dream bigger, and do not let fear or doubt hinder you.

- Every time we changed our fishing spot, Pastor Randle and my husband pulled up the anchors and dropped them in the new spot. *Life Application:* Sometimes life can weigh you down. It is nice to have friends who will help you lift heavy loads, especially as it relates to ministry. Also, it's very important where you drop your anchor (where you settle in ministry). Allow God to lead and guide you.

- We caught enough fish to eat until we were full, and we took fish home. *Life Application:* We all went fishing with the same goal … to catch fish. We were not competing against each other. We encouraged each other and was happy every time a fish was caught, regardless of who reeled it in. God wants us to be the same way in church regarding ministry and outreach. We should all strive to be supportive of each other and have the common goal of sharing the gospel to reach the lost.

We first met the Randles last year on a life-changing mission trip to Africa. However, after our fishing experience and quality time spent with them, we feel extremely blessed and honored that God is using us to support and encourage each other to continue to serve God's people with honor and integrity.

I cannot wait for my next fishing experience. I will definitely pray for more than one fish, and I am sure I will again receive a lot more than fish.

Kaitlin Janay Randle

My daughter, Dr. Kaitlin Janay Randle, a twenty-five-year-old physical therapist and resident of Dallas, Texas, shared a fishing experience on November 15, 2020 with Pamela and me, where we witnessed her catching her first fish. She had this to say:

I was filled with anticipation on the car ride over to the fishing pond, although a bit nervous and unsure having not been fishing before. I asked, "So what professional advice do you have for reeling one in?" My dad started to answer, and I jokingly interrupted and said, "Oh no, I was talking to Mama, the pro." We shared a good laugh over that one.

My dad then offered me a quick read-through of one of the unedited chapters of his book. As I read through the chapter titled "Fishing the Tight Line," I began to understand the different ways to reel in a fish. I read on the different ways the fish will bite on the bait and how to react as the fisher to successfully hook one. This translated quickly from reading in the car to sitting in the boat with a fishing pole in my hand, my dad to my left and my mom to my right.

We had not been fishing very long when I felt a small tug. Confused about whether it was a bite, I waited. I watched the tip of the pole carefully to notice any small movements. Then suddenly, there was a larger movement, and I figured that was my chance. I tugged hard in a backward motions and began to reel in. It was lighter than expected, and unfortunately, I came up empty-handed. My parents gave me a few pointers. They said, "When you feel the pull down, that is your cue. Then tug upward rather than backward." I thought about the body mechanics that would entail and mentally practiced it. Not very long after, I felt more action. This time I waited. I felt a small pull down, and then suddenly, I felt the big one. I immediately tugged up on the pole and began to reel in the line. This one was much heavier and harder to reel in. I knew I had him. I stood up to get a better handle on him. At the same time, my dad stood up to record the action on his phone. As the fish broke the plane of the water, there I was, staring at my first catch—a catfish—with a huge smile on my face, might I add. My dad asked me how it felt to catch my first fish, and honestly, it felt great. The act of practicing patience, combining sight and feel, and perfect timing all playing together so beautifully felt great. Not to mention I had the first catch of the day! It was an unforgettable moment, sitting on the boat with my mom and dad, in the middle of the pond with my first fish moving around in the cooler I was sitting on. I will never forget it.

Freddie Banks and Jayvyn Banks:

A Day They Shall Never Forget

The best thing that a father can do is to give his children, especially his sons, a fishing experience.

Minister Freddie Banks has been an acquaintance since childhood and the first member to join the Lighthouse after its inception. He was also highly instrumental in the formation and foundation of the church. Though I no longer pastor Minister Banks and his wife, LoIita Banks, I consider myself fortunate to have afforded Minister Banks an opportunity to share a first fishing experience with his son on a boat on November 25, 2020. Minister Banks had this to say:

Fishing and Fellowship

> Train up a child in the way he should go: and when he is old, he will not depart from it. (Proverbs 22:6)

> While on a fishing trip with my former pastor and now family friend Pastor Allen R. Randle Sr., I was asked, "Minister Banks, do you still hunt?"

> My reply was, "Well, sir, not as much as I used to." After some short dialogue we went back to how we both got interested in two different sports. Pastor Randle

stated that his dad would take him fishing, but they never did much hunting. So that is why he enjoys the sport of fishing—besides the fact it relates so much to soul winning. Then I shared that my dad never took me fishing or hunting, but because I knew that my dad enjoyed hunting, I took up the sport and learned from friends later in life.

Now why is this so important? Because at the time of this conversation, my twelve-year-old son was experiencing his first fishing trip with two prominent men from his community who are influential in shaping his life. He will always be able to look back at that day that he drove a boat for the first time, caught his first two fish that got away, and spent time being trained as a child to grow up to be a productive citizen in the sportsman paradise. This training will further dispel the myth that pastor's kids are bad kids. I know for a fact that the three children from both our families are well mannered and heading for success according to God's plan for their lives.

Jayvyn Banks, my twelve-year-old "play" nephew, had this to say concerning his first fishing experience on the water:

> This experience was a very exciting one. Before we started, we prayed for safe travel on the waters. My father and I learned how to launch the boat. After we got on the boat, I learned how to drive the boat. It was really nice. Then I technically caught two fish, and my father caught one. The ones I caught did not make it into the boat before they fell off the hooks. It started to rain, so we had to wrap things up. Afterward, Pastor Randle let us keep the fish that he caught. It was a very nice gesture of kindness.

ALLEN R. RANDLE, SR.

First Lady Pamela D. Randle

Don't Let the Red Bottoms Fool You: A Personal Testimony

The Feeling of Reeling One In

Not unlike the feeling you get when you are reeling in a catch of the day, reeling in a soul for the kingdom feels just as exciting. I will never forget the feeling of catching my first fish. I had gone out previously on our boat for a scenic joy ride with my husband and our two children. It was my first time on a fishing boat. I am accustomed to cruise ship–sized boats, so I was not quite sure how I would like it. Needless to say, I enjoyed it immensely. But I still was not ready for a fishing expedition. You see, I am a girly girl, and the thought of being outside in any type of elements does not appeal to me at all. I do not like heat, and I definitely do not like bugs of any kind. What does appeal to me is being inside, whether inside the house, inside a restaurant, or inside a mall—just inside. My husband would go out fishing a couple of times a week and was so joyful every time he returned. He loves being one with nature and was secretly hoping that I would one day join him on the water. As joyful as he was upon his return trips, I still was not interested.

Approximately six weeks after my scenic joy ride, I decided to join him on a fishing trip. Of course I told him I would have to get all the necessary "girly" attire, which included a pink fishing pole and matching life vest along with other color-coordinated attire. He was just excited I wanted to try it, so he was all for my getting whatever I thought I needed. As the morning approached, I was starting to feel a little excited. I could not tell if the excitement stemmed from the anticipation of fishing for the first time or putting on all my new fishing attire.

It was probably more of the latter, or so I thought. He started me out top-water fishing. For those wondering what that is, it entails fishing with a stopper (called a bobber in some parts of the country). Once the fish takes the stopper down into the water, the fisherman jerks the line with hopes of snagging a big one. That form of fishing did not quite work out for me.

I could tell my husband did not want me to get discouraged, so we moved to another spot, and I tried tight-line fishing. Tight-lining is a little different; it takes more of a concentrated effort. You have to watch the line for the nibble. Once the fish is attracted to the bait on your line, the fish will come around and try to remove it. Just as in fishing for souls, we have to make sure our bait is attractive. I have learned in fishing it is all about the presentation. The nibble of my first fish was exhilarating. But I jerked the line prematurely, and it got off. We must be careful as Christians to not prematurely scare off the nonbeliever by being too aggressive in our approach. I had to learn how to feel the nibble and then wait for what my husband calls "the takedown." Once I felt the bend in my rod, it was time to jerk. The feeling of the weight of the fish on my line and reeling it in was like nothing else I had ever felt.

My husband was so excited for me, but at the same time, he wanted me to take my time and enjoy the moment of bringing one in. That feeling actually made me reflect on the first time I went out witnessing for souls when I lived in Galveston, Texas. That was a new experience for me as well. I was going into uncharted territory, much like my first fishing adventure. I eagerly anticipated what would happen out on the streets of Galveston with my witnessing partner. We were armed with our four spiritual laws tracts and a lot of determination. We knocked on several doors. Some never answered, and some were simply not interested in what we had to say. You see, as with fishing, you will not catch them all. Some of them will get away no matter how good the presentation is.

I will never forget one particular house we visited. I was anticipating another rejection, but instead, this young woman listened intently to us. We were not overbearing; we just simply offered Christ to her and showed her how to bridge the gulf between her and God. She accepted Christ that day as her personal Lord and Savior. My heart raced with excitement for her over the fact that I had gotten to take part in leading someone to Jesus. I said earlier that reeling in my first fish was like nothing I had ever felt, but it still could not compare to winning a soul to Christ. That is the greatest feeling in the world.

I have since graduated to a "real" fishing pole, and by the time this book is published, I will have purchased an even better rod and open-face reel. You see, I started out in the beginners' category, but I have advanced rather quickly. Just as with fishing for souls, start where you are and allow God to advance you to the next level in winning souls.

Who would have ever thought …

- I would go from looking for the perfect pair of red bottoms to looking for the perfect fishing boot.
- I would go from shopping for the perfect designer outfit to shopping for fishing attire with the right amount of SPF in each piece.
- I would go from making sure my makeup was just right every time I left the house to just throwing on a tinted moisturizer to head out the door to go fishing.
- I would painstakingly make sure my natural hair's curls were popping to throwing it in a top knot so my fishing hat would fit OK.
- I would go from not liking the outside to finding the beauty in being in nature on the water—though I still don't really like the outside.

Who would have ever thought …

- I would go from someone uninterested in church to being a first lady who not only has a passion for fishing for fish but most important, for fishing for souls.

Do not misunderstand; I still like being a girly girl and looking fierce. But don't let the red bottoms fool you. Fishing is now one of my passions, and I truly believe that God ordained it to be so, so that I could really understand the correlation between fishing for fish and fishing for souls.

CONCLUSION

There is one final piece of business for all fisherman. Do not forget to purchase a fishing license. Underaged children are exempt. A fishing license may be purchased at a low cost at a local Walmart store or at the Department of Motor Vehicles in most states.

The license needed to fish for souls is found in Matthew 28:18–20:

> And Jesus came and spake unto them, saying, All power is given unto me in heaven and in earth. Go ye therefore, and teach all nations, baptizing them in the name of the Father, and of the Son, and of the Holy Ghost: Teaching them to observe all things whatsoever I have commanded you: and, lo, I am with you alway, even unto the end of the world. Amen.

Just as the fisherman must carry the fishing license when fishing the waters, the same applies to the fisherman for souls. Since fish are always biting and there is a need for the fisherman of souls to fish at all times, Matthew 28:18–20 must be carried at all times. This license is permanent and will not expire until Jesus returns to receive all the fish caught by faith and the gospel.

Most states have limits on the number of fish a fisherman of fish can catch. There are also restrictions on the size of the fish the fisherman can catch. However, for the fishermen of souls, there is no limit on how many souls can be caught for the kingdom of God. Furthermore, there are no size restrictions either. I encourage all fishers of men to catch souls in great numbers regardless of age and size.

Go get 'em!

To pastors, their wives, and church leaders—
For small- or large-group seminars, conferences, or workshops on fishing for souls, or for a REEL experience on the freshwater lakes in south Louisiana, please call 337-578-7243.

A

R—Relaxing
E—Enjoyable
E—Evangelical
L—Learning

Experience

ABOUT THE AUTHOR

Allen R. Randle Sr. is a native of Baldwin, Louisiana, and is happily married to Pamela Denise Randle. They have two godsent children: Kaitlin Janay and Allen Ray Jr. Prior to becoming the founding and organizing pastor of the Lighthouse Missionary Baptist Church of Franklin, New Iberia, and Abbeville, Louisiana (one church with three locations), he coached sports, was a private baseball instructor in South Houston and Galveston County, an English teacher at Galveston College in Galveston, Texas, and the youth pastor of the Macedonia Missionary Baptist Church, also in Galveston, under the leadership of Pastor A. W. Colbert.

Printed in the United States
by Baker & Taylor Publisher Services